It's Not Where You're From
But Where You Wish To Go

It's Not Where You're From But Where You Wish To Go

Peace

George W. Burnette III

George W. Burnette III

To order additional copies of this book, contact:
Xlibris Corporation
1-888-795-4274
www.Xlibris.com
Orders@Xlibris.com
86402

CONTENTS

WHY THIS BOOK

The known lineage of George W. Burnette goes back to his great-grandfather George W. Burnette, Sr., who was born a slave on September 17, 1851, in Covington County, Alabama, and who passed away on December 3, 1903—the same year my father was born. Most of his lifetime was spent in Crenshaw and Covington counties, where records show that more than twenty-five thousand slaves existed.

I have little information about his life as a slave, but I do know that early on, he was exposed to Sacred Harp music, probably because he had the duty of driving the wagon to church at the plantation where he worked. My great-grandfather would sit at the back of the sanctuary with other slaves during church singing hymns and, as a consequence, learned how to sing Sacred Harp music.

Benjamin Franklin White and E. J. King from Georgia are credited with publishing *The Sacred Harp* in 1844. They used a system of four shapes to help singers recognize notes. They are a triangle (fa), a circle (so), a square (la), and a diamond (mi). The major scale is this four-shape system expressed as fa, sol, la, fa, sol, la, mi, and fa.

THE SACRED HARP

First published in 1844, *The Sacred Harp* songbook has helped to promote the style of singing known as "Sacred Harp," "shape-note," or "fasola" singing.

(Reprinted with permission from *The Atlanta Journal-Constitution*)

The Osgood File (CBS Radio Network): 9/3/01

> Antique American religious music enjoys new national revival.

> "Amazing Grace" originated as a Sacred Harp song. Sacred Harp refers to the human voice or "the harp you were born with," and it's a type of religious group singing from the late 1700s and 1800s. This antique American music form was adapted from 18th century English church music. Sacred Harp became the first music to develop among the colonies and took hold in the South. Today, in addition to traditional Southern singings, 23 states host Sacred Harp conventions, some of which draw hundreds of people. Nationally circulated newsletters and Internet lists of singing events keep singers and fans informed of Sacred Harp activities across the United States.

> The sound of Sacred Harp singing has been described as a cross between Gregorian chanting and bluegrass. People hearing the music for the first time often describe it as

"harsh" or "eerie." Singer Jim Carnes says that to the modern ear, Sacred Harp music can "seem a pungent medicine." It's a melancholy sounding cadence and form of music, and the voices don't blend as they do in, say, a barbershop quartet, but participants say it makes for a real community experience—social, musical and religious. (The Osgood File)

Sacred Harp is also known as "shaped note singing," because it is written with notes that have four distinctive geometrical shapes (a triangle, an oval, a rectangle, and a diamond) to facilitate sight-reading.

The four shapes in Sacred Harp music represent the four pitches (notes): fa (the triangle), so (the oval), la (the rectangle), and mi (the diamond).

(*The Osgood File. CBS Radio Network 9/3/01*).

The most popular songbook, called The Sacred Harp and originally published in Georgia in 1844, continues to be updated and used today. Sacred Harp music is based on hymns and religious subject matter. Some of the songs are based on psalms and scripture, moral lessons, expressions of faith, and the thorny topics of sin, doubt, death, and judgment. For believers, the songs are an expression of their religious faith. But for an increasing number of people, including members of other religious, agnostics and even atheists, Sacred Harp has become increasingly popular simply for its aesthetic appeal.

People attend Sacred Harp singings for the religious and spiritual appeal of the music, along with the strong family and community feeling that develops, according to Sacred Harp historian Buell Cobb. He says the combination of many different melodies, harmonies, strong rhythms and powerful singing—with everybody letting loose—makes for a powerfully moving experience. It's one of the rare occasions when even people who are not musically gifted can sin "all out." Cobb says it's a physical feeling to be buffeted by other peoples' voices, and it's not uncommon for people to burst into tears from the power of the experience.

From this exposure to Sacred Harp singing, a dream was born. My great-grandfather realized he was so carried away with this music, he purchased a small farm on top of a hill. The farm was a level piece of property that was purchased by my great-grandfather and other ex-slaves, and on it, a Primitive Baptist church was built. Sacred Harp music has been sung by every generation from then until the present by the Burnette line.

The church that the freed slaves created was similar to the church they had attended when they were slaves. Everything that took place at the Primitive Baptist church was based on their experiences in the former church. One of the great similarities was the after-service noon dinner, open to all. Our great-grandfather developed a sauce to put on goat meat, which was a crowd favorite. After more than 150 years, this basic recipe is still being used by his descendants. George W. Burnette III prepares this food for his church each first Sunday after Communion at Hillside Presbyterian Church, in Decatur, Georgia.

George Senior also made sure that his love of Sacred Harp music was passed on to his children and his children's children. It is amazing how they learned this music even though there were no schools to train ex-slaves. To add to the difficulty, two of his children were born blind yet still learned to sing Sacred Harp music. We were exposed to this music as young children. We rode the wagon each Sunday to attend Sacred Harp singing events. We began doing this at a very early age, as babies.

For about ten years growing up, I had the truly amazing experience of watching Uncle Dove and Aunt Catherine sing though they were blind. What was even more amazing is that Uncle Dove would pitch the tune himself. When I consider all the things I failed to do as a young person, this stands out as my greatest omission. I learned a few notes, but I could not plow from Monday morning until Saturday night and then sing on Sunday—I just didn't have the energy. My parents and other relatives attended church to sing Sacred Harp music. This type of singing went on from the end of slavery until 1948 in the Primitive Baptist church.

Sacred Harp singing, which began after slavery and continued at the Primitive Baptist church until the summer of 1948, then stopped. The older members began to die out, and no one was singing or learning it. For three years, no singing took place at the church our great-grandfather helped to build. After three years of no singing at this church, the land was purchased and a lodge hall was built to be used by Prince Hall Masons.

The few singers in the Crenshaw and Covington areas began to spread out of these counties. These members began to reach out to other singers in Ozark, Troy, and Enterprise, Alabama, where another tradition also had started during slavery. The tradition that began after slavery is still going strong today. This was a great day for my great-uncle and my father. They could see the tradition that had begun after slavery continued on for future generations. These elderly members, who had gone on before, would be shouting in the graves to know that this tradition is continuing and growing stronger each year.

In Montgomery, Alabama, they have the rotunda singing at the Alabama State Capitol, where they sing from the *Sacred Harp*, 1991 edition. The second is from the Alabama Christian Harmony. The third session is from the *B. F. White Sacred Harp*, Cooper edition, and the last book used is from the The Colored Sacred Harp. Last year was the twelfth edition of this singing. It is growing stronger each year. It is the wish of our ancestors that this type of singing never ends. I will be making the trip each year, as well as my grandchildren. The history of how Sacred Harp got started and the part my great-grandfather played in its development—this music touched their hearts and souls. It is hoped that this will be an inspiration for the young members of the Burnettes to keep the memory of our great-grandfather until the end of time.

INTRODUCTION

The First Epistle of Paul the Apostle to the Corinthians was not an easy letter to write, but its author knew it would be even harder to receive. After sending it, he was beset with misgivings concerning the effect it might have on his relationship with the church, where he had labored so long among friends he so deeply loved. But he could not wait in quiet or inactivity; he must go on to Macedonia, where he met Titus returning from Corinth. When he learned that his letter had been received in a spirit that recognized his authority, and that his injunctions concerning the offender had been obeyed, his joy was so great that he immediately wrote his second letter.

It is my fervent hope that I will be invited back to speak at another reunion.

At an installation service at a sister church last Sunday, Dr. Allen McSween preached from the fourth chapter of Second Corinthians, and his sermon was entitled "Tell them the truth." That is what I am going to do tonight—tell you the truth.

Speech, Burnette Family Reunion
August 16–18, 2002

Good evening, my kindred visitors and friends of the Burnettes, on the occasion of our celebration of the Burnette lineage at this thirty-third family reunion.

I am glad that I have an opportunity to address this family celebration of our remembrance and history.

In Exodus chapter 4, God spoke to Moses and told him to take his shoes off because the ground on which he was standing was holy ground. If our ancestors could speak to us tonight, they could say the same to us.

The site on which we are standing could very well be called hallowed ground because it is here where many prayers were lifted, sermons preached, hymns sung, feet washed, and I might add, Sacred Harp songs were sung for over a hundred years by the lineage from which we come . . . and that's what I want to talk about for a minute or two, Sacred Harp singing and how it is linked to our heritage and why we should do everything within our power to preserve it.

Sacred Harp or four-shape or whatever you want to call it, of all the talents possessed by the Burnette family, Sacred Harp singing is our spirit, our soul; it was poured out many times right here where we are standing. It is a great talent that is fast escaping the Burnette family. If we are going to have true connection to our heritage, this is a talent that must be revived, learned, and passed on to the next generation. It is very easy to say "I can't sing" and forget it. This is no excuse to let a great part of the Burnette heritage slip into history. The spirit of our ancestors should cause us to spend time each day practicing notes and teaching our young. When we sing, we should remember and recall the courage, faith, and moral strength of those Burnettes who have gone on before us, who are a great cloud of witnesses looking down on us, as excuses are made for our failure to live as true servants of our heritage. As I look around at the attendees here this evening, I wonder how many of us are old enough to have sat here in the sanctuary of that Primitive

Baptist church and heard the great tenor voices of George Washington Jr., Arvester, Uncle Sam Daniels—not in our lineage—Uncle Dove and Aunt Catherine singing joyfully even though both she and Uncle Dove were blind. I was blessed to sit and hear the lineage of George Senior unleash their burdens through song—Sacred Harp—that we now wish to abandon and let it disappear in the wind.

Just think. They learned this music even though many of them—two could not see—were barely literate. This music helped them to persevere during difficult periods we can't imagine as they toiled and struggled to earn a livelihood as they labored daily from sunup to sundown in the vineyard of American life.

Before I make my next point, I want to quote a passage from a speech by a great American given on September 19, 1913, in Nashville, Tennessee, to the National Baptist Convention . . . We had been free fifty years.

One thing stands out . . . clear and distinct in the way of achievement during the last fifty years. We black Americans have proven to the world that we can survive, from a physical point of view, in a state of freedom. There were not a few who predicted more than fifty years ago, when the Negro was made free, that he would disappear as a race. At the beginning of our freedom, we numbered four million. After fifty years of freedom, we now number over ten million (1913), a population larger than that of the whole of Canada and twice as large as that of Australia.

We have not only survived but we have also proven to the world, from an economic point of view, that we could support ourselves. There were not a few who predicted before our freedom began that we would prove, as a race, a perpetual burden on the pocketbook of the nation, that we would not clothe, feed, or shelter ourselves.

During all the fifty years of freedom of our race since the days of reconstruction, we have never called, as a race, upon Congress to provide for a single dollar to be used in providing food, clothing, or shelter for our people. And this is the point emphasized . . . We have not only done this but we have also accumulated something over $700 million worth of property upon which we pay taxes in this country.

How did our ancestors exist without government? They formed mutual aid societies or unions as they were called. They helped each other with food, clothing, and medical bills and prescriptions. The providers were paid after the monthly meeting, which was usually the first Saturday of each month.

Now, the bombshells.

There is the problem of teaching our people how to keep and use property in a way not to injure the value of that property, but to increase it. In too many cases, when a Negro family enters a dwelling, it seems that very soon the palings from the fence begin to disappear, that very soon the gate is off the hinge, windowpanes disappear, and old pillows and sheets take their place. All these injure the reputation of our race and makes life harder for us . . . The problems the speaker lamented in 1913 are, sadly, with us today . . . The homesteads of our ancestors have disappeared into the trees or replaced with trailers . . . You may be wondering who this great American I have been quoting from is . . . It was Booker T. Washington—founder of Tuskegee Institute.

If the American dream, as some of our black leaders would have us believe, is now a thing of the past, at least it once existed; and Booker T. Washington, born a slave, a Negro, the humblest of the humble, once made that dream come true. And he did it by devotion to virtues that no longer are extolled as highly as they once were—the virtues of cleanliness, godliness, thrift, perseverance, hard work, and honesty.

If a person came to this country today from overseas, they would not know Booker T. Washington existed because his name and accomplishments are never mentioned during Black History Month celebrations in the schools.

I want to say to the parents of young children, get a copy of his book *Up from Slavery*, read it and have your children read it. Paperback copies cost less than $4. Check with Willie Mitchell Burnette, over at alumni affairs in Tuskegee University, Tuskegee, Alabama. He may be able to get you copies for less.

Let us resolve this day to reach back into our heritage and draw on the insights and the hardships our ancestors endured and gain the prominence they envisioned for us and not let them down. The society appears to be crumbling around us, and we are swamped with taxes to fix problems in society and our school. America doesn't have money problems; we have moral problems. Do you think that the decline of marriage and the dissolution of the family is just a money problem? Or do they come from putting self first as if there are no obligations that have to be respected? Does freedom mean nothing more than licentiousness, than stupid self-indulgence? Those of our ancestors who toiled in the depths of slavery know that the bestowal of moral dignity on everyone is the great gift of America, not making mountains of money.

They did not tell us that freedom would be an easy road. They offered us a true vision of the promise of America, the future of our legacy, the future of the principles that guided their lives as they sang Sacred Harp songs and prayed for a brighter day for us.

What have we come to? Our children are not being educated. How can they compete in a global economy when third world children outscore our children on most tests in math and science, the two main subjects that our children need to be proficient in order to train and be employed in the technological age? We don't seem to care; our sons' hair resembles women's, and rings are in their tongues, ears, and noses. Their trousers are dragging to the ground. We don't act as responsible parents; we are more like hosts. Look what following the crowd has brought us . . . a dismal future. We have found ourselves at a crossroads and do not know which road to take.

This is an occasion then for the Burnette family to declare to the world that we accept the challenge of helping to prepare our young people for the journey they must take to keep the fires of the Burnette legacy and traditions burning in the future.

This family then should liken itself to the old man—as the poem goes—who was building a bridge across a wide and treacherous stream when he was interrupted by a voice nearby.

Old man," said a fellow pilgrim near.
"You are wasting your time building here.
Why, your journey will end with the ending day.
You never again will pass this way.
Why build this bridge at evening tide,
Across this chasm, deep and wide?"
The old man lifted his gray head and said,
"My good friend, there cometh after me today,
A fair-haired youth, whose feet must pass this way.
Though this chasm has been as naught to me,
That fair-haired youth, a pitfall it might be.
He too must cross this chasm in the twilight dim.
My good friend, I am building this bridge for him.

So, my kindred and friends, we must look back at the bridge we have built for those who will come after us to cross and reflect on our contributions. What is our history—are we happy with the chapters we have written? What kind of memories and legacy will the Burnettes have to say about us, this generation in 2030? Will they say Uncle Hassan or Aunt Timika were great Sacred Harp singers, or will their remembrance of our history and accomplishments be blank pages?

It is time now for someone to learn how to make fish baskets, make spade hogs, make cotton baskets, make barbecued goat like Uncle Boy or a fine wine from blackberries, muscadines, or grapes like George Washington Jr. or Arvester or piece a fine quilt with multicolors. The thoughts of these and many other talents—George Junior pulled teeth and Arvester cured the thrush on many children black and white—remained with me as I traveled almost the entire globe as a soldier for more than thirty years. The talents possessed by members from the lineage from which we come could fill a very thick book. I wish someone would begin writing before all the knowledge has left this generation.

I have been trying for more than twenty-five years to recreate the recipe for barbecue sauce like Uncle Elliot used for goat and ribs and a fine sipping wine for communion. You might say that I have been somewhat successful in these endeavors. Not to brag, but I won my second first place award last November at the Hyatt Regency hotel in downtown Atlanta, with Arvester's wine recipe and Uncle Elliott's recipe for barbecue sauce. I was interviewed by one newspaper and declined an interview by a reporter from the *Atlanta Journal-Constitution*, a cable television channel. I received numerous requests to cater events for as many as 1,200 persons. The talents and skills possessed by the Burnettes, if applied today, we could own and operate very lucrative businesses, employing hundreds of people and enriching ourselves in the process.

So you see, my kindred, what we are doing here during the celebration of the Burnette legacy is lighting a pathway for our youth to follow for generations to come. We must remain firm and resolute in this undertaking, or our legacy will blow away in the wind.

In closing, let me say that the yoke that has been placed on our shoulders to carry on the Burnette heritage is heavy. We can shoulder the load and move forward with pride in our ability to carry on the legacy or succumb to failure. We have, as has every generation of Burnettes before us, the privilege of looking like Moses into the Promised Land. If we return to our heritage with its moral principles, devotion to citizenship and service, and a strong, abiding faith in our Sacred Harp music and the Almighty, we can pass on to our children we see and those we cannot see that the true heritage of the Burnette legacy is our real responsibility . . . Let us not leave the great cloud of witnesses wanting.

Peace be with you.

Good afternoon, my good Christian kin and all the other visitors at the annual George W. Burnette Sr. family reunion. It is indeed a great honor to be here. I say honor because I had to undergo my third procedure on my heart in January. So you see just how honored I am to be with you today.

I left home at the age of eighteen to join the army, so many of you don't know me. I may ask you your name to see if I know you or your parents.

I want to speak with you for a moment on the occasion we are celebrating, the Burnette family reunion. We are celebrating the heritage of a great man, George W. Burnette Sr. George W. Burnette Sr. was born a slave somewhere in this county. I am still working on his lineage so at some point I can give you his full heritage.

As a young slave, one of his duties was to drive the slave owners to Sacred Harp singing. This exposed him to Sacred Harp singing, and it remained with him until the slaves were free. It really touched his heart, and it stayed there.

Somehow, he convinced other freed slaves to help build a church. If you were at the fish fry last night, you stood on the site where the church was built. It was a Primitive Baptist church. This is the same kind of church he drove his slave owners to. It left a great impression on him. We have let it slip away. There are many reasons we have let the tradition slip away. We failed to hear the music from our parents. They tried to teach us, but we thought we had more important things to do. And here we are today with our hands outstretched, searching for answers. As I make these comments, I traveled all over Georgia and Alabama trying to learn this music. This is a tradition I don't want to see slip away in the wind.

All my brothers and sisters have books and tapes. I would venture to say that none of these tapes have been listened to or songs practiced.

We have five grandchildren—all of them have books and tapes. This is not a family thing; it's for all Burnettes in this generation.

Most of the singings I attend are in the churches of a person who have gone on before us. We sing in this person's memory. That is what I want to do as a tradition to George W. Burnette Sr. I want to look at this book and see the memory of George W. Burnette Sr. come alive.

I attend Sacred Harp singings all over Georgia and Alabama. Most of the time, I am the only black person in attendance unless my spouse accompanies me. I want my great-grandfather's memory kept alive.

My eldest brother was attempting to bring Sacred Harp music back as part of the Burnette family heritage before he passed away ten years ago. I am now picking up the tradition he was trying to reestablish.

I invited singers from Elba, Enterprise, Andalusia, Goshen, and from towns in Florida to put on demonstrations at our annual family reunion in 2007. All these singers were white. I have provided all my brothers and sisters with books and tapes, and we have all made a commitment that this part of the Burnette heritage will not blow away like the wind. My grandchildren have been promised a college scholarship funded by me if they learn Sacred Harp music and attend church.

When I was younger, we sang, but not Sacred Harp. We had a group called the Burnette Brothers and Bud, who was a second cousin. We practiced for over a year, but we never did perform. We would practice but would not sing. They were afraid to stand on the stage and sing to the congregation. We were trying to do anything to make money. If you were really good, you could earn up to $25 after each performance during church service if you charged a fee. To this very day, I regret not learning Sacred Harp music. Now in my old age, I travel all over Georgia and Alabama trying to learn this music. I hope someday to have a memorial day for my great-grandfather and conduct an all-day singing somewhere in Covington County in Alabama. He could not read or write, but he taught his ten children this music, bought a farm, and built a Primitive Baptist church there.

My Memories

I, George W. Burnette III, was born on November 10, 1933, on a farm owned by the Wells family, in Crenshaw County, Alabama. We referred to these farms as plantations because they were very large. One must assume that these plantations had slaves because they were so large. Several families lived there. The house I was born in was the longest house in the area, so we had plenty of room. It was the house where the slave owners once lived when slaves worked at the plantation. It had a walkway to the kitchen, which was separate from the main house. The house for the slaves had been torn down. In some locations, there were a few old buildings out in the woods—some of these were allowed to deteriorate.

My family lived on this farm for four years, but the work was too much for the one mule we had for plowing—we needed five or six. My father, with the help of two elder brothers, tried to train a bull that would assist the one mule we had, but training a bull to plow was very hard. He had gotten the idea from his aunt Rebecca, who trained a bull to plow after her husband died and she couldn't afford another mule. My father's bull was named Tupin. He was wild and wooly. They would begin plowing, and the bull would run away. They would catch Tupin and get him to plow a few more rows, and then he would run away again. They tried for over two years to train the bull to plow. The family gave up trying to train the bull to plow and moved to a large plantation in Luverne, Alabama. Mules were expensive. During this period, it was not unusual for a farmer to pay over $500 for a good-quality mule.

After my great-aunt Rebecca became a widow, the owner of a large nearby farm came to see her and made a promise to take the farm if she lost it to foreclosure. After her husband died, we would plow our fields and then help plow her fields. We even helped her pick cotton. Our great-aunt sold eggs, fruits, figs, and anything that would make a profit. She did absolutely everything within her power to pay the farm off, and she did. She shouted when it was done! This land and farm is still in the family.

After trying for two years to train Tupin to plow, we moved to a large farm in Luverne, Alabama, owned by the Horns. We did not want to leave the Wells plantation, but in 1935, we found it necessary to move for two reasons: first, it was near a farm my grandfather had farmed, and second, the owners of this plantation owned twenty-five or so mules that we could use for farming and plowing. This plantation had both white and black farmers. The owners were also in law enforcement. Their family members rotated between being sheriff and deputy every four years in Crenshaw County. This process lasted more than fifty years. During their tenure, I had two uncles convicted, who served four years and fifteen years in prison. They did not spend their time in prison; they were paroled before their time was up. In 1954, the Horns lost the election to a new sheriff who received almost the entire black vote in the county. The new sheriff went out and sought the black vote and was elected. These voters were tired of the autonomy created by the Horn dynasty in law enforcement. When I returned home from the army in 1955, the new sheriff was on duty in Crenshaw County.

The first year of our move to the rural area of Luverne, the husband of my mother's eldest sister died. We boarded a Trailways bus in Luverne and rode to Brantley, Alabama, where Uncle Lidge met us at the bus stop and took us to our aunt Melzie's house. On the way there was a certain tree stump, where my uncle stopped and removed a bottle of corn whiskey and took a sip. I guess it was a tradition that the older men knew where the moonshine was kept. Later, a truck came by and picked up Uncle Thomas's body for the funeral services at the church. I was four and my brother was two. From my early youth, I always heard good words about Uncle Thomas and what a great man he was. He was a great leader and served as a deacon at Spring Hill Baptist Church, even as a teenager.

In the summer of 1937, a truck came to Luverne from New York to recruit men for employment in the steel industry located in the Buffalo and Niagara Falls, New York, area. I remember that day very well. It was a sad day for the girls because at 5:00 p.m. or 6:00 p.m. on a Sunday evening, that truck left for New York with a truckload of men they had recruited in Luverne. I thought the young girls would never stop crying.

My mother had a record player. She got this record player when property was divided after her father and mother died. The older people would listen to records of Blind Boy Fuller while they danced on the front porch. If the attendees needed dental work, our grandfather would pull their teeth even though he wasn't a dentist. I often think about my great-grandparents and wonder if they wanted their son, George Junior, to go to school and become a dentist. If he had gone to dental school, he would have been one of the first black dentists in the county. My grandfather had foresight, but he never owned any land. I have often wondered why my great-grandfather's children did not follow his lead by purchasing their own farms. They all elected to become sharecroppers on large plantations. None of the boys owned any land—only one aunt and her husband, whose farm is still in the family-owned land.

Our grandfather George Junior was an industrious man; he had many talents. He was an expert on timber products and had a reputation for making quality railroad cross ties. He had a contract with the railroad to cut cross ties for railroad tracks. He had a quota for each of his sons. Each had to cut twenty cross ties each day. When the company sent someone to inspect the ties, the inspector would start writing when he saw my grandfather on the cross ties because he knew he was an expert. No inspection was necessary.

Our grandfather, George Junior, had vehicles during this time, in early 1910 to 1920. He drove Model Ts. That was George Junior's specialty.

While my grandfather took care of teeth, my grandmother was a specialist with burns. People would come from miles around for her services, and she helped many people. My youngest sister is one example. She had a large burn on her face. My grandmother cured it after three months. One of my sisters was ironing some clothes and was accidentally struck in the face. A doctor tried to heal her but was unsuccessful. Our grandmother treated the scar and cured it in less than three months.

Other family members followed my grandparents' example. My mother's sister was an expert in children's illnesses. Late in the fall of the year, she would pick herbs and weeds that she used in her cures to make medicine. As a child, I never saw a doctor because of my aunt's services, but her expertise wasn't just limited to relatives. I recall a white family coming to our house looking for my aunt's house. They said that the doctor had given up on their child, and they were hoping my aunt could help. My father gave them directions, and she treated the child. Months later, we saw the child's family. The child had been healed by my aunt Melzie.

My father was also recognized for some medical knowledge. He cured thrush on both black and white persons all over Crenshaw County. We only lived in Luverne for one year. Our father did not like the financial setup with the Horn family. The Horns wanted half of my father's farm and half of his crops of sugarcane, potatoes, etc., which was excessive. So he found another farm in the south of Brantley, Alabama, owned by the Rains family. The Rains family owned a very large farm. It ran all the way to Conecuh River and over the railroad tracks.

Aunt Rebecca was next in line to receive the syrup mill after our great-grandfather died. She was married to a very fine gentleman who wanted to own his own land. When Aunt Rebecca passed away, our father was next in line to inherit the syrup mill. In order to inherit it, you needed to own land to put it on. After many years of sharecropping, our father finally got the syrup mill on four acres of land that he purchased near Spring Hill Baptist Church, where he retired as a deacon for over forty years.

While living at the Rains plantation, our house caught fire. Our eldest brother, Pete, saved the day by climbing a ladder and putting the fire out. Mother had left our elder sisters Mary and Nellene in charge of making dinner that evening. When the stove overheated, a fire started on top of the house. I thought my sisters would never learn to cook. They would make bread, and if it turned out bad, they would give it to the pigs. Sometimes the food would be so bad, even the hogs wouldn't eat it! The elder sisters finally learned to cook, and it was really great to have good food all the time.

After moving to the Rains farm, the one mule our family owned died. We then had to use the mules owned by the Rains. After a year or two at the Rains plantation, our father found another farm three miles away that had a different crop structure. We had one mule, and the owner had several mules. My brothers plowed the owner's mules while our father plowed our mule.

Since two of my great-grandfather's children were born blind, they lived on the farm with him. When he died, Uncle Dove stayed on with his mother, where he remained even after her death. Aunt Catherine, Uncle Dove's sister, move in with Rebecca, their elder sister. Being blind, Uncle Dove had access to people with writing skills and other skills related to farming and how to make a living.

Somehow, Uncle Dove developed a relationship with a young woman who lived some distance away. After a year or two of corresponding, they met at the train station in Dozier, Alabama. I understand that he described his financial setup and landholdings to be quite substantive. In any event, the young lady, who was not blind, was interested enough to come to Dozier. She arrived on a train, and they met. Later, she met the minister and members of the Primitive Baptist church and, that evening, ended up marrying Uncle Dove in the church that his father had helped build.

Our grandfather was very skilled. During his life, he learned how to spay hogs and cows to keep them from reproducing. This skill did not help veterinarians as it took away their business.

In 1937, construction began on U.S. Highway 29, which runs from Washington DC to Florida. Some of the more experienced workers moved their families nearby if they could find housing. Since some of their children did not have to pick cotton, they were the young students I walked to school with each day. However, some of the workers that followed the highway construction let their wives pick cotton and work on the large plantations. Everywhere we lived, the plantations were very large.

I began my education in 1939 at the Macedonia Elementary School in Brantley, rural route. The school was located in a Baptist church. Since this was a rural area, the older children picked cotton, and the younger children were able to attend school. Things went well at school until the older students started arriving after harvest around the middle of October. At 5:00 p.m., I would pick cotton with my mother and father, but only in the evening after school. At age six, I was given a large sack for picking cotton.

We were in a one-room school with one teacher, Ms. Hill. She would continually speak to the boys about their conduct. I wondered why she kept mentioning student conduct. It turned out that the older boys were pinching the girls on their behinds or reaching over their shoulders to rub their chests.

On the third day, after continuous disobedience by the boys, Ms. Hill became upset and lined the boys up near the stage after lunch. She pulled two or three large switches from the back of the stove and began whipping the boys. I sat, terrified, in a front-row seat. She continued to whip them, and I sat there and relieved myself; I was so afraid.

Occasionally, she would stop and say, "The next time I'm going to whip the fire out of you!" I was so scared that I got my bags and went home when school was out and never returned even though I turned six on November 10, 1939. I spent a lot of time thinking about the teacher and what would happen if fire came out of those boys! See how stupid I was to believe that fire would literally come out of the boys?

First Grade—The Second Time

We moved to the sports plantation in 1940, and I returned to the elementary school in the fall. I had the same teacher I had at the elementary school in 1939. I returned to the same elementary school in Brantley, Alabama. The school was still in the same location, at Macedonia Baptist Church. I began classes in 1940. Although I was only in the first grade, I would come home after school and go straight to the fields to pick cotton or take water for the workers to drink.

Ms. Hill spent 1940–1942 there before she left for another assignment. She was very tough. Her favorite comment was that she was "very tough" and that her name was Hill because you needed a tack in your shoes to climb her. I don't know how long she was there, but she was truly a dedicated teacher.

I learned to read and write under Ms. Hill's tutelage. After she departed, I really missed her. During her last two years at the elementary school, I missed her dedication. If your homework was not turned in, she would whip you. In her last two years, I did not ever get a whipping for not turning in my homework assignment on time.

While living at the sports plantation, some of the older members formed a union. The union was used to pay doctors for service. If you saw a doctor, the union paid the bill. This same union also paid for your funeral if you died. Our father became the treasurer of the union. He kept the records and collected the dues. I don't know how our father became the president, but he was very efficient. The union met once each month. This union was started after slavery, and it was still going strong when I entered the army in 1952.

I recall our father coming home after attending a union meeting. He would tell our mother, whom he saw at the meeting. If some of the men would be high on spirits, our father could smell it on their breath and tell them what they had been drinking and then drive them home. Our mother could also tell. She could tell them if the moonshine they had been drinking had been "run too early" and what was wrong with it.

Our father had to learn how to make moonshine at an early age because it was his father's recipe. As a young child, he would spend days at the still where moonshine was made. He learned this skill and became very proficient in it. I wished many times that our father would work the land. Instead, he became a great winemaker. He could be in the record books today for his wine-making skills.

Second and Third Grade

In the fall of 1942, a new teacher was assigned to our school. The war had broken out in 1941, and my two eldest brothers were drafted in 1943 and 1944. Even though I worked in the field, I would give seeds to the planters and distribute fertilizer for the cotton, corn, and peanuts. Sometimes my father would allow me to plow, but not for a whole day. I did this many times, but my main job was to be water boy and fertilizer distributor for planting and chopping cotton.

When my last brother was drafted in 1944, I was given his mule to plow that winter while my father plowed with the other mule that we owned. The owner had hired workers to plow using the remaining mules. As I mentioned, this was a very large plantation situated between two major rivers—the Conecuh River and Patsaliga Creek. We plowed well over one hundred acres even after my brothers went into the army.

In the spring of 1945, when I was handed a mule to plow, I was briefed on how to feed the animals. There were nine or ten mules in the barn. I was shown the feed and instructed that the person placing the last mule in the barn had to feed all the others. I was usually the last one to get my mule to the barn because I farmed the backfields.

We began plowing that spring, and I was given my own mule to use by the owner of this large plantation. I recall plowing for six straight weeks and did not see school. I would lie awake and wonder or say a prayer and wonder what was going to happen to me if I never went to school again. I wanted to be higher than fifth grade. I actually prayed for it to rain so I wouldn't have to plow. I was lost and did not know what to do.

On that Sunday night at the beginning of the seventh week, it began to rain. It was too wet to plow. I went to school for three days because of that. We didn't have a library, but there were a few books and a dictionary against the wall on a shelf that our uncle Lidge built. One of the books was about great Americans. I would read from this book between classes. What really caught my attention in the book was the entry about Abraham Lincoln: how he would split rails all day long and study at night by lamplight. After reading his story for the second time, I thought I would do the same thing. After plowing all day, I could study at night. This was my starting point. I studied every night from the fifth grade until I finished high school. How I finished high school, I do not know. I knew very little, so I had to study all the time.

Everybody at school had to bring their lunch. Even though this was a one-room school, we had to fill the stove when it needed wood and pick up the paper. After we had lunch, we had to clean up the yard.

We had no cafeteria at this elementary school. Everybody had to bring their lunches to school. Even then, as poor as we were, we shared with students who didn't have anything to eat. We ate outside under the trees, but there were no benches. Later, a few benches were built and donated to the school.

After lunch, the teachers lined up all the students in a straight line to police the area for paper and other trash. I walked around the track at a high school this morning and observed all the trash and bottles all over the grass. As I walked, I kept asking myself why, in this day and age, we can't pick up after ourselves. We did this in the first grade at the small elementary school I attended in 1939.

Many young students did not finish elementary or high school. The books we had were used books, and you had to cut wood for the school. Sometimes the parents would cut the wood, but that was rare. Our elementary school had a very large heater near the front of the classroom. We would stand by the stove until we got warm and then move back to our seats.

Occasionally, some of the children would come to school without coats. The teacher would send a letter home to the parents telling them that the attire wasn't sufficient to keep the student warm. Even though we were poor, somehow, the parents would find coats and jackets for their children. Many times, the kids would come to school and forget their coats. If coats were needed, they were donated by many of the elders in the community. During this time, the older parents would share clothes for needy students. Our teacher was very resourceful and got donations from many older members of the community who didn't have children.

Some days it would be too cold to do much classroom work. At that point, the teacher would write to the parents, asking for help procuring wood for the stove. This usually got a response from the families that lived near the school.

The elementary school had a PTA program. The members usually met at the school after classes were over while their children waited for them. Most of the members were women because the men were working. Occasionally, a few men would come to the meeting if they did not have second jobs and had the time.

Uncle Lidge and our cousin Mack Mitchell were farmers. They did not work at the sawmill like some of the fathers. They were older men and more stable financially. They survived on the earning from their farms. They also owned cows and hogs that they sold in the markets every year.

During my time at the elementary school, there were only two families that had hogs and cattle to sell. My family occasionally had five or six pigs or a cow to sell, but it was rare. My father had to work year-round to provide for our family. When the crops were all gathered, he would work at the sawmill. At night he sharpened the saws for the mills on a stand he made. Sometimes he would be filing saws at eleven o'clock at night so that they would be ready the next morning when the truck picked them up.

My father did this until 1951, until we were old enough to pick cotton and earn enough money to get us through the year. The few potatoes we grew were also a bonus that we took to the market in Montgomery for more income. You had a limit on cotton, so we planted potatoes to supplement our income.

It was great to look at the bank statement and see how much money we had. We even got a newer used car, paid for in cash from our farm earnings.

In the spring of 1946, a line was run through our community to bring electric lights to the community. But the lines only ran to the homes of the white families living on the plantation. No blacks got electricity. My mother said this was our sign to move, but my father wouldn't hear of it. There was no reason we did not get lights. This was a private company, but the whites did not want us to have lights. The owner of this very large farm wanted to raise cattle. He began taking, little by little, more and more of our land; eventually, we were told to find somewhere else to live. We moved two years later to a much-better farm. By the time I was sixteen, we had two plow mules that we actually owned.

When the soldiers returned from the war, they had different plans for farming. After a while, my father saw the handwriting on the wall and quickly began looking for another farm. My mother tried again to get our father to purchase a farm. He wanted a place, but it had to be near the sports plantation. Mother never stopped begging Dad to buy a farm, but she died never having had a farm.

Fourth Grade

After school in fourth grade, I plowed all day. We had to do all our chores first and then eat dinner and shell peanuts to plant in February and March during planting season. After all this was done, you had to study at night. There were many nights where I was tired, but I still studied. I made up my mind that I would go beyond the fifth grade. This desire gave me the energy to keep studying.

Return from New York

The workers who were recruited from Luverne for steelwork in New York in 1935 came home in 1937 after two years for a vacation. They spread the word that they had found paradise. People began to leave in droves. I remember one family had cotton in the field, but when they heard about how great things were in New York, they left their unpicked cotton and headed north. It was 1939. The original landowners, their great-grandfather, purchased the land after they were freed from slavery. My great-grandfather did also. The site where my great-grandfather and church members built the Primitive Baptist church is in this area. Our great-grandfather's land was a half mile from this site. When Sacred Harp was no longer popular, the church was torn down and replaced with a Masonic Lodge. For more than twenty-five years, we hold the annual fish fry at this site during our annual reunion. A lot of history is associated with this place. At the Primitive Baptist church, they would do foot washings annually. This was a great tradition that took place.

Seventh Grade

I continued to study at night until I completed elementary school. The elementary school was in Brantley; the high school was in Dozier.

This was a change. We had walked to elementary school about three miles each way.

From the fifth grade until I was promoted to the tenth grade, we only had kerosene lamps for lights. This poor light began to affect my eyesight. In 1949, we moved to the Boykin plantation, where we had electric lights. I was really happy because I could study at night with good lights. I really needed those lights because my vision had begun to suffer. We had five teachers for grades 7 through 12 in Dozier. This was a high school, yet there were only five teachers. The principal at this school was very resourceful. We had great PTA programs. The PTA paid for our annual trip to Luverne. I was a junior in high school when I transferred to Luverne in the fall of 1950.

When I could attend school, the students in my classes were always amazed at what I knew. Whenever I was called on by the teacher to respond to a question, I always knew the answer. I knew the answers because I was studying at home at night.

During the winter of 1939, just before Christmas, we moved to the sports plantation. At this plantation, there were two more children born into my family: in 1940 and in 1943 was when my youngest brother and sister were born. After this, no more children were born. We now had eleven children.

Learned to Swim

We had a lot of free time in the summer when we moved to the sports plantation. We spent this time fishing with our mother. Our mother loved to fish. Father worked at the sawmill during the summer and winter months. Often we would be joined by some of the white youth who lived on the plantation. They taught us to swim. They would bring their fishing poles and fish with us. Usually, they would give us their fish. We ate a lot of fish during the summer months.

We would start off in the shallow area of the creek. Two years later, we had moved into the larger area of the creek, which was as deep as in the pond or lake. The whites had a nice pool in Dozier, but it was off-limits to blacks. We kept close association with these white families for ten years, and after more than sixty-five years, my younger brother still has contact with them. They voted my brother, Vick, mayor of Dozier for term in 2008.

We walked six miles to and from the elementary school. At Dozier, we rode in a used bus when it rained. While working on the farm, we would often quote from ministers we had heard preaching on Sundays. We would discuss their language, especially if it was bad or they used "broke" verbs. This amusement was used often after a revival or meeting at church. If the minister or other leader used improper language, we had to comment. This was our way of describing their actions.

One elder brother was discharged from the service in 1945 and the second brother in 1946. It was great to see them again. They had the GI Bill but never used it to further their education. Our mother prayed for my elder brothers while they were in the army and even harder when they came home. She could not understand why they didn't want to advance their education in order to improve themselves.

Dozier High School was in Dozier, Alabama. I attended school there until I completed the tenth grade. During this period, they completed a large high school in Luverne, Alabama, and they made the high school in Dozier a middle school. The high school was tenth through twelfth grades for students from Dozier, Rose Hill, St. Luke, Mulberry, and other places. This school was called Crenshaw County Training School.

High School in Luverne

We began attending Crenshaw County Training School in the fall of 1950. For the first time in the history of Crenshaw County, black students were given two new buses—but we still had the old buses too. The buses were for the students that had to ride twenty to thirty miles each way to reach school. I and the other students were very happy because our buses were new. My bus went from Searight to Luverne, Alabama. We made stops in Dozier and Brantley on the way to Luverne.

We had different teachers for several classes. We had a science teacher, civics teacher, and teachers for math, English, social studies, physics, and chemistry. It was really great because there were several teachers who had specialties, such as chemistry. That was exciting because it allowed us to expand our study disciplines.

The English teacher was great, but Mrs. Campbell had serious coughing spells that would sometimes last most of the class period. This really hurt me academically because I was already missing so many days from school when I had to plow instead. When she taught, she was truly outstanding. She came to Crenshaw from Alabama State although she was originally from Arizona. She said she had won a large college scholarship, which she used to attend Alabama State University. She often talked about that: how much money she had received and how she had gotten requests for donations from various churches in the Arizona area.

During the new school year at the Crenshaw County Training School, we had to pay for the senior class prom. We could also attend the prom as eleventh graders, but I didn't go. I didn't go to the prom because I did not have a suit to wear.

During my final year at Crenshaw, there were a few boys who always had money. They would sneak off campus and purchase spirits in town.

I had been absent from school for a few days, and when I returned, I saw the senior boys after one of their trips to the spirits shop. Class was being held in the library, and they entered with the smell of alcohol on their breath.

The librarian went to the principal, who promptly suspended the entire class. I raised my hand and told him that I had done nothing and that it wasn't right to send me home. Then some of the other good students started speaking up for me. He didn't send me home, but from that point on, I almost had to walk on eggshells because I had embarrassed the principal. In spite of this incident, he allowed me to graduate with my class in May 1952.

One of my brothers started classes at Crenshaw after I did. He was in the tenth grade. He ran with the city boys, flunked out, and was not promoted. When he failed to get promoted to the eleventh grade, he dropped out. He finally finished school after he broke his leg at halftime playing football at Dozier High School. When he was healed, Papa visited the principal, and he agreed to promote him if his schoolwork was good. Consequently, my brother was promoted to the eleventh grade and eventually finished high school in 1954. At this time, I was seven months from leaving for the army, in December.

What I really liked about the new Crenshaw County Training School was the books. In elementary and junior high school, we had used books from white schools; but at Crenshaw, we were able to purchase brand-new books from the bookstore in the city of Luverne.

During my last two years at Crenshaw, the principal put in place a code that one day in a week—usually Friday—you had to dress up. I wore the same trousers every Friday that I attended class, but that wasn't too often because my family would begin plowing in February and wouldn't stop until the crops were laid in July. So I didn't spend many days in school. If we went to school, it was usually between planting corn and planting cotton. We planted corn in March, cotton in April, and peanuts in late April or early May. We also planted sugarcane, potatoes, and beans.

During the summer months, our job was to take water to the fields for our father and the other planters and farmers. Later, we had to cut wood after they had cut down the trees. My brother and I used a large crosscut saw to cut the logs for firewood for the stove and the fireplace.

We also picked cherries and berries for canning and figs for preserves. We had to do this every summer after the plowing ceased around the Fourth of July. This was the time for my father to pick the first watermelon of the season. Our father always planted our crops using an almanac. He even butchered hogs using the almanac. He used the almanac each season, even for spaying hogs.

When we completed all our tasks, we went fishing with our mother. We also played baseball during the summer. We had a very fine team. I played my entire career under one manager as well as three elder brothers. We played baseball in the summer when the plowing was finished. I thought I would sign a contract the last year; I was really good. Scouts would look for players, and they came the year I went into the army. My two other brothers were very good. My brother Joe pitched in the Negro League for the Indianapolis Clowns in 1958 and walked away from a contract with the St. Louis Cardinals the next year. When the baseball season was over, he came home with a few hundred dollars in his pocket and got involved with a young woman. He didn't want to leave her at home pregnant, so he married her but was definitely a Big League player.

The scouts from the Cardinals really wanted Joe on their team; they sent numerous certified letters to his attention. Joe was a great pitcher, and he had the potential to make it in the Big Leagues in two years. He walked away from a great career. After nine children, he and his wife divorced after twenty-two years.

On the Fourth of July, my great-uncle would cook a feast and sell food during the annual baseball game. He carried on this tradition for more than seventy-five years, using a family recipe handed down from his grandfather. We continued to enjoy his food until he passed away in 1965. This was a great tradition because during the Sacred Harp singing performance, they served our great-grandfather's famous barbecue sauce on goat meat. I went to a family reunion in 1969, and there was no barbecue because my great-uncle Elliot had passed, and he was the last to know the recipe for the sauce.

But I still had three great-aunts, so I began corresponding with them, trying to rediscover the recipe. So after ten years, I thought I had gathered enough information and ingredients to try to replicate the sauce. I was partially successful; it's still not how he prepared the sauce, but it is close. I have actually won awards at major cook-offs in Atlanta and twice have been sponsored in contests by the Atlanta chapter of the 100 Black Women of America.

It was really great to come to Dozier because in addition to Uncle Elliot's barbecue chicken, ribs, and camp stew (a stew made of tomatoes, beef, pork, and several other ingredients), we had a great baseball team. A lot of people came to see us play baseball, but a lot came for the barbecue sauce and camp stew.

When we finished plowing around the Fourth of July, I got a job at a sawmill in Highland Home, Alabama, in 1951. The owner would not pay the wages he was paying the other workers. They received $6 per day; he paid me $5. He changed his mind when it came time to start picking cotton again. Then he offered me $6 per day. He knew what a good worker I was. I said no and returned to help my parents gather the crops.

The owners of this sawmill was the Kimbrough family. You could hear them talking about employees and how they were performing the work at the mill. This was the fourth mill I worked for during the summer months. I began working at sawmills at the age of fifteen.

After sharing with my parents, I saved my earnings under the bed until January because Father would go to the Army Surplus Store and buy clothes for us to plow in. The place where we bought our plow clothes was in Rose Hill, Alabama. While I was at the store, I saw a suit with a price tag of $5, so I took $5 from my savings and bought the secondhand suit and had it cleaned. This was the suit I wore to the prom. I don't know why we went to the prom. My cousin and I had no dates, so my father dropped us off at the prom entrance with me in my $5 suit.

Three girls were standing at the prom site entrance. One of the girls had dropped out of school and had a baby and returned; the other two were just homely. My cousin, being the eldest, agreed to escort the girls inside since we would otherwise have had nobody with whom to dance.

The prom went well though there was no orchestra or band, just a record player and not many records at that. They kept playing "One Mint Julep" most of the evening.

After it was over, two carloads of students were driven to Troy to take the college entrance examination. I was not selected to go. I guess the staff and the principal decided who had the potential for college.

Later, after I enrolled at Tuskegee Institute (after I had left the army), I attended a basketball game at Alabama State University and ran into two girls from my class who attended college there. They were not included in the group that took the college entrance exam in Troy, either. Both were juniors; I was a freshman.

We received our final grades in 1952 and were told that we would graduate. I told my parents, and for two weeks, they discussed my graduation gift. My parents were proud because out of eleven children, I was the first male in my family to finish high school. My mother wanted to get me a new suit. After much discussion, I got a new suit, which I still have hanging in my closet today. This suit cost $24 in 1952.

Now I had two suits: the one I got for prom and the one for my high school graduation. I ordered two pairs of jeans and two shirts from Sears in Atlanta with the money I had earned that summer. I also ordered four sets of underwear. These would have been my school clothes if I had gone to Tuskegee at that time.

Graduation was a very big deal. I was the first male in my family to complete high school. I made a big issue out of it, and my mother made it into a big occasion. I was happy because my mom was happy. She would compare me to my brothers who did not use the GI Bill to further their education.

She was hoping that I would go to Tuskegee using the five-year work/ scholarship program. We spoke about it several times, but our father let the dream die by denying the proceeds from the cotton that he had promised my brother and me for plowing that spring and summer.

Every spring since I was in the sixth grade, my father promised my brother and me a gift for working hard each summer. The promised gifts varied each year; it would be goats, pigs, a cow, or a bicycle. The year 1952 really stands out in my mind, though. My father was very elegant with his promise that year. Father marked off some land and told us that we would be given the proceeds from this parcel after the cotton was picked and sold.

However, during the entire period from sixth grade through high school, Father never kept his promise. When the time came to get a gift, he would make an excuse. We worked for nothing all this time except for a decent living with good food to eat. Even today, I still make fig preserves to keep my mother's memory and my grandmother's memory alive. From time to time I eat and share them with members of my church, clerks at the bank, people who play bridge with my wife, and some of my doctors and nurses.

I was so happy that I wrote to Tuskegee in 1952. They responded by sending me a college catalog and admissions application for the five-year work/scholarship program. The cotton was picked and sold. That Saturday morning in September, my father got us up early and took me and my brother Vester to the state motor vehicle division to take the test for a driver's license. I said, "No, Papa. I don't want a driver's license. I am going to Tuskegee." I think my father knew he was not going to keep his word about going to Tuskegee because he kept insisting that we get our license. I passed the test and got my license that day. The next day, my father gave us each $20 and told us to wait until the following year when we would then be able to buy a farm from what we had saved from the previous year. I saw the statement from the bank. The money was there.

The funds we had been promised blew away with the wind. I walked to Dozier and got a ride over the river to St. Luke for church service that Sunday. I sat there during the service listening to what the minister was saying. I sat there thinking about my father's promise. My thoughts went back to the Presbyterian minister from Selma, Alabama, who spoke at our baccalaureate ceremonies. He spoke about controlling your destiny. I was very disappointed, but my anger never showed.

The baccalaureate program had been a great experience. The minister was very specific, and his language was perfect. He preached about the destiny that we all have. He spoke of the hardship one would encounter along the road but how we should never be deterred.

I found myself writing down almost everything he said. Through the two or three remaining days at school, I continued to think about his message. It was like he had been talking to me personally. I had asked myself many times where I was going and what I should do to reach my destiny.

The next day, I returned to plowing the field. I often said that if the county had a plowing context, my dad would come in first, but I would come in second. At the Boykin plantation, we lived next to U.S. Highway 29, and people would stop and watch me plow. They would be amazed at how I controlled the plow and how straight the rows were.

After the cotton was picked and sold, we began to cut trees for poles for the peanut crop. After that, we started to gather the corn. That Tuesday morning—I will never forget—the harness on one of the mules broke. Since I had my driver's license, my father gave me money and sent me to Luverne to buy a new set of harnesses for the mule. This was the first time I had driven the car since I got my license.

I got the harness and was on my way back to the car when I stopped to look at an army display that had some weapons that had been captured in Korea. One of the soldiers asked me why I wasn't in the army. I told him that I was waiting for the draft because I only wanted to be obligated for two years. My plan, after the army, was to go to college.

At that point, the soldier's partner spoke up and told me that I could go down to the draft board and volunteer and still only get two years' service. I left there and immediately volunteered.

The dearest friend I ever had joined the army on August 29, 1952. He got a three-year enlistment. I guess he didn't know that he could have volunteered and gotten two years. I knew if you volunteered for the air force, you would have to do four years. That was out of the question. It was also four years for the marines and the navy. I didn't know that if you volunteered, you could get two years. I told a few friends what I had done, and no one wanted to follow me.

We knew nothing about the army or how long the enlistment period was. Usually, recruiters would visit the schools, and we could learn about the services from the visitors. Nobody ever visited our school. A lot of fellows wanted to join the air force, but they would not be accepted by the recruiters. Three young men went to Niagara Falls, New York, and joined the air force. Both of these men did almost thirty years in the air force and retired. One of these soldiers retired and lives in Las Vegas. We visited them in 2004. We were third cousins.

I returned to the field and resumed harvesting corn. I never told my father what I had done. I continued to gather corn and peanuts. In about thirty or forty days, I received my notice to appear for my examination for military service in Montgomery, Alabama. Once I found out I had passed, I asked if I could leave immediately. That request was denied because the next draft day wouldn't be until January. It was now before Christmas, and I had three weeks to wait. I wanted to leave immediately because my sisters would be coming home for Christmas, and I wanted to leave before they came. Instead, I was there at home when they came.

They asked my mother why she looked so sad, and she told them about my being drafted into the army. At that point, I was given a lecture by both of my sisters. They asked why I was called up ahead of so many older guys. I had to admit that I had volunteered. I then received another lecture and was told that I was a fool, a big fool.

They wanted to know how I got the idea to volunteer for the army. I told them about the Presbyterian minister who spoke about controlling your own destiny. They responded that my destiny was a pine box, and for the life of them, they couldn't understand why I would listen to a preacher and follow his advice.

I didn't sleep well that night. All I could think about was a disaster happening in Korea.

Fall 1952

In October 1952, after I had volunteered for the draft, my great-uncle, Uncle Sellars, came by for his yearly visit to our house. He told us how much money one could make picking oranges in Florida. I had volunteered for the draft but would not be drafted immediately, so Uncle Sellars convinced me to accompany him back to Florida to pick oranges in many of the large groves in the Dade City area.

My goal was to earn and save as much money as I could while down there, and I ended up with $100—I was there for two months. I could pick cotton but not oranges. I was really glad I could not pick enough oranges to pay for school and was glad that while I was in Florida, I received my call-up notice in December.

I passed my exam and reported for active duty on January 14, 1953. When our processing was complete—at Fort Jackson, South Carolina—I became ill. I became ill because it was freezing, and the clothes I had were insufficient for the cold weather in South Carolina. I was eventually hospitalized for seven days. We received orders to attend medical corps training. I missed this assignment because I was in the hospital. I was headed to Korea as a medic. The military then assigned me to another branch. It was the infantry division for Korea, a second time. During infantry training, all I could think of was an air attack by the enemy. I had these feelings almost every night; it became worse the closer I got to the end of training. I don't know about the other soldiers, but all I could think about was what I would do if we were attacked by the enemy. I would think about my sisters. All I could do was think about what they would be saying about my volunteering for service. I had to volunteer because there was no way for me to go to college without the GI Bill. I had no funds to pay what was required for the five-year work/scholarship program. These funds were required for one month's tuition, room, food, and books. This would have cost me three hundred dollars. I had earned it, but my father changed his mind, and the only way I could attend was to volunteer for the army.

Military Duty Overseas

After two months overseas, I began as a military policeman after two senior master sergeants gave me two weeks of intensive training. I had learned from my first cousin that if a soldier were dishonorably discharged, he would not be eligible for the GI education bill. Thus, I was motivated to do my best while in service. I tried to stay away from people who didn't care to succeed.

I did make mistakes, though. Once I went to town with several soldiers who became unruly around midnight. One soldier had become frustrated with a young lady who did not want to be bothered with him, so he stood up and said, "Let's tear this town up!" I left with a couple of other soldiers before the military police arrived but realized I had almost been caught up in the incident.

This was a turning point in my military career. All the way to the office, I was really worried that I might be in trouble and they would end up putting something in my record that would lead to a dishonorable discharge. Soldiers were picked up—some of the soldiers were not from our unit. Some of them did time in the stockade in the southern part of Germany. I escaped this incident with no marks on my records. I learned a very good lesson that evening. There were a lot of ways one could get into trouble. From that moment on, I did not get a demerit, or gig, as it was called during inspections.

About two months later, we had an inspection, and my gear and clothes were perfect. I had passed the inspection with flying colors. The first sergeant told me that I was being transferred to another unit—an all-white unit that had been called to active duty during the Korean War. This was a National Guard unit with members from Ohio and Pennsylvania. I was the first African American in the unit at the time.

A lot of the guys in the unit had attended or finished college, and some had jobs in the industry. My platoon leader was a senior at Ohio State University. They would get mail from home, but mostly it was newspapers like the *Wall Street Journal* or other financial sources. After they had finished reading them, they would pass them on to me. Sometimes I would wait until they were away and then read them.

I didn't understand anything in the financial articles, but the others didn't know it. They would talk about stocks and bonds and other investments and how well they were doing financially. I really missed my old unit, but I did not want to go back. I found out that several of the guys in my old unit had been placed in the stockade back in the States and were doing time at Leavenworth, Kansas. These were really bad soldiers.

These new guys were giving me a whole new perspective. These older soldiers talked about the real-world experience.

During my free times, I would study in the library. I kept my nose clean and did not do anything that would put a mark on my record.

A year later, we received several new recruits. Five were black—one from South Carolina, was married with a family. He was older and was a steady influence on me. I had put in a year of service and still had not made private first class. Yet I was a good soldier. The married man was from Florence, South Carolina. We are still in contact. He is retired from the post office. His first wife died, but he is happy with his second wife.

Some soldiers in our unit could not read or write. One of them was from McComb, Mississippi. Once, when he was on duty, he received a letter from a young lady in Mississippi. He came to me to read it to him and then asked me to write her back. I did, and several days later, she apparently responded but I didn't read it. The soldier had found somebody else when I wasn't available to read the letter for him.

He came to my room when I got off duty and threatened to "whip me up" about the letter. He was upset because she accepted his proposal for marriage when he returned home. Apparently, he did not want a spouse. I came to find out the hard way that his purpose was only to hold on to her because he was not the marrying kind. I also learned that he drove a 1950 Buick, and many of the young ladies of McComb, Mississippi, ran after him because he worked for the largest funeral home in McComb. After this happened, he never asked me to write for him again.

He was a very tough young soldier. He had no schooling, but his brother in the Twenty-fourth Division had gone to school and was a very sharp soldier. I met him twice before I returned to the States. Unfortunately, the illiterate brother ended up doing a long prison term at Leavenworth. He was one of the soldiers with me in my old unit, before I was transferred to a new unit.

This young man from McComb was a good soldier, but he had a bad temper and he liked to date—a lot. On one occasion, he brought a young German lady to a movie on post. He lit a cigarette, and they asked him to leave the theater. He started an incident. He got a thirty-day suspension. On the last day of his suspended sentence, he went to town and was seen by someone from our unit. He was picked up when he returned to the base. He went down the hallway, and when he saw one of the guys that reported him, he hit him with an entrenching tool. For this, he got three years. We were at the movies to watch *From Here to Eternity* featuring Burt Lancaster.

My unit has a very effective security system for prisoners, but once we had a prisoner escape three times in one day. After his third attempt, he was scheduled to be put in the cell block but had to have an examination first, per policy. At that time, I was the only guy on duty. The sergeant gave me the task. While the soldier was being examined, I was joined by another soldier to assist me at the hospital.

After he was examined, we were escorting him to the cell block, but he broke free and ran. He was shot. After that, we had mounds of paperwork to complete about the incident. The next day, I had to see the colonel who was the commander of the stockade. I was overseas in Europe. I was nervous and even thought I might get court-martialed. All I could think about was what kind of discharge I would get.

When I reported to the colonel, he looked at my appearance, then he asked me how long I had been in service. I told him that I had put in fourteen months. He asked me my grade and seemed surprised that I was only a private, not a private first class after fourteen months.

That day, he called the company commander and asked him about my lack of promotion. He then told the commander that he was impressed with me and wanted me to be promoted that day. I received a promotion and a job change. My new job gave me twice the amount of time to study, and I took advantage of it.

Once, while I was away on escort duty, the platoon sergeant picked up the mail for me to make a mail call. When I returned, he asked me if I was trying to go to college. He said he noticed all the mail I had received from several colleges that I had written to.

I told him about my goal of using the GI Bill to finance my college education. He said he was proud because I wanted to improve myself, and he wanted to help me. He then asked me about taking college entrance tests. I hadn't taken either the SAT or ACT because I knew I wasn't ready, and I had not yet applied to college. The sergeant took me to the library and found books to help me prepare. I ordered the study books before I left the military in 1954, and I had these same books when I arrived at Tuskegee Institute in the fall of 1955, when I went to enroll.

The president of the First National Bank in Dozier, Alabama, lent the $1,200 I needed for my four years at Tuskegee ($300 for each year). My final year, he didn't require a cosigner. He just let me have the funds. I was very fond of this man because of the vision he had for my success. I was probably the only black person from Dozier to whom he granted an educational loan. When I reached Tuskegee that Sunday evening, I almost left. The students were talking about courses I had never heard of, and I felt extremely intimidated.

That Monday, I took the entrance exam and passed. I wanted to shout! I could not control my emotions, so I went into the bathroom and cried and prayed. I was a very happy man. I was very happy because I had taught myself to pass the entrance exam while in the service. I had studied for it for more than two years in the army, and it paid off. The next day, we began registering for classes.

My initial plan was to major in building construction, but the required math classes caused me to change my major. Why I was afraid of the math, I don't know. Maybe it's because I thought about the principal at my high school who told me that I was not college material. My thought went back to that destiny the Presbyterian minister talked about seemingly so long ago. I decided on social studies and English.

I thought about what the preacher said at my high school; I knew I did not know enough about math to take this chance. The major I chose required me to take two classes in math. We had two classes in math the first year—Math 101 and Math 102—and one math class in the sophomore year. All together, I had two math classes my freshman year. This was all that was required for a degree in social studies and English. My grades for math and English were so low that I did not know enough about either of them to pass any course. I ended up taking math three times and English for three years. I also took history two times.

After one year, I was put on probation for two years. All I could do was study. I was hospitalized three times from exhaustion during the four years I was at Tuskegee. After the last time, I decided to quit school. I actually did quit.

The military science professor told me that I would be out of ROTC at the end of the semester if I didn't pass my history exam the following Monday. That really hurt. I had come to Tuskegee for ROTC. I studied for three days before the exam and took it with the class. On the Wednesday of the week of the exam, I got the results; I had made a D. I was frustrated and angry and decided to leave school for good.

I caught a bus and ended up in Montgomery, Alabama. I had been sick all day and hadn't been able to eat anything. All I could think about was that Presbyterian minister and wonder why I was foolish enough to follow his advice.

I went to the military recruiting station in the city but didn't volunteer. Around midnight, I caught the bus back to Tuskegee. To this day, I don't know why. I got my books and returned to campus. On the way back to campus, I walked in the middle of the street—figuring that a car would hit me and it would all be over.

No cars passed, and I was back on the campus. I sat down by the Booker T. Washington gravesite and prayed. My roommate, Joseph Agee, from Point Clear, Alabama, was away on an internship, so I had the room to myself. Joseph Agee was a great student; he left the army as a lieutenant and went to California. He was a builder.

I made the decision to study until I dropped dead and they would take my body back home for a big funeral. It helped me to attend chapel and listen to the choir when I was low in spirit. Their music would bring me back. I don't know how I would have made it without that great choir. I think the best choirs at Tuskegee were the ones in 1957 and 1958. They were good every year, but these were the best. I listen to their tapes now and think about how I struggled back then.

We attended chapel three times per week. In the spring, we had Religious Emphasis Week. I must add that we had some of the greatest ministers in the country conducting our services—ministers such as Dr. Howard Thurman, dean at Boston University, Dr. G. Taylor from New York, John Hope Franklin, and Dr. Benjamin Mayes from Morehouse College.

Each night, the Tuskegee choir would put on a masterful performance. I would often think of my grades and how they were too low to allow me to join the choir. Singing in my family goes back to slavery.

I was not allowed to belong to any organization because of my low grades, but the dean of the English department asked me to join the Little Theater. To join the Little Theater, you had to have a 1.5 GPA. My GPA was .92, and I did not have a prayer. I didn't go to the tryout. He sent word to me, and I still did not go. A few days later, he confronted me in the academic building and demanded that I show up at the 7:00 p.m. rehearsal that evening. I told him about my grades, but he was the dean of the English department and ran the Little Theater.

When I got there, he gave me the leading role in the annual play. *Mister Woodruff* was the name of the play. That was the only time—other than my ROTC photo—that my picture appeared in the annual yearbook.

I attended summer school 1957–1958, studying night and day. I took a full course load. When summer school was over, I went home to help my parents pick cotton. One day the postman came with a letter from Tuskegee. I was afraid to open it, but it contained good news. I had been removed from academic probation.

I was a happy man! I was so happy, I couldn't stop picking cotton. I was energized. I had thought so many times that I would drop dead; now all my hard work was slowly paying off. I was readmitted into the ROTC program. I could keep my head up and smile at the other students. That was a great feeling to walk to classes with your head held high.

At the end of this very happy week, I received a message from a friend that the father of a young lady I had met before I went to the army wanted to see me over the river at Pigeon Creek. I wondered why the father wanted to meet with me. I knew that I had never touched his daughter, and she was not at home. Believe it or not, some young ladies would get pregnant as a way to get to go to Niagara Falls, New York. This young lady, however, was not pregnant.

I caught a ride over the river and met the father. We talked for a while, and then he showed me his land and then his logging truck in the barn. When we got back to the house, he told me that he liked me and he wanted me to marry his daughter. Tears came to my eyes, but then I told him that I couldn't do that. I had made progress at school finally, and I couldn't let anything interfere with that.

I later went home and told my mother about his offer. I thought she would say I should have taken the offer since we did not own any land or property, but she supported my decision. I was happy twice. My path was clear, and all the land and the logging would not get in my way.

I returned to school and continued to study the same as always and made sure I excelled in the ROTC program. I became platoon leader at the beginning of my last year at Tuskegee and ended the year as executive officer of the battalion. This showed my leadership, but they did not commission me in the combat arms.

My senior year, I wanted to attend the ROTC ball, but I had no one to escort. So I put out a message to anyone who might want to go, and I would come over to look at the gowns of any interested junior or senior girls each Friday evening.

The ROTC ball was one of the great traditions at Tuskegee. The ball was one of the highlights on the campus. We would have soldiers coming to our ball, and they would bring their dates or wives. We would have other students from other schools visiting Tuskegee for the sole purpose of attending this ball.

I ended choosing neither a senior nor a junior, but a young lady who had a very pretty gown. She was a sophomore. At the dance, the cadet colonel danced with the ball queen. I was the executive officer of the battalion, so I had to dance with Miss Tuskegee. After that, I danced with the young lady with the gorgeous gown. I never saw her again after that because I had not tried to date her.

Graduation for the winter term was held on May 25, 1959. I did not graduate because I still had my student teaching to do. I had been accepted for a position with the public school system and had been assigned to a school about a one-and-a-half-mile walk from the Tuskegee campus. I taught English during the first part of the day and social studies in the afternoon.

My roommate for the summer term was Nathaniel Frazier. I had to study in the library because Frazier had a record player and two albums. One was "Take Five" by Dave Brubeck and the other was by John Coltrane. Frazier played them in the mornings before work and in the evenings after work.

I completed my student teaching and received two Bs, one for each term. I passed my grades on to the registrar at Tuskegee and received my permission to graduate on August 14, 1959.

My next move was to Montgomery to purchase the military uniform I would need after graduation. I ended up purchasing two uniforms: one for summer and one for winter, as I was reporting in February 1960. There was a store that sold uniforms on credit, so I let them see my certificate to graduate. I waited while the uniforms were altered and then picked them up and returned to Tuskegee.

When I reported for duty at Fort Benjamin Harrison in Indiana, they paid me my clothing allowance, and I sent the store the balance I owed on my bill. I wanted a career in the military. That was what I had made up my mind to do before I left Tuskegee. I loved the military and wanted to be an officer. I had found out how one could become an officer. Prior to enrolling at Tuskegee, I would read records of outstanding officers during my off-duty time, at the library. I would try to pattern myself after them, but my lack of education held me back. Upon entering the army after college, I had to study day and night to keep up—this was due to lack of training in the school system because I had to work year-round on the farm.

That Friday, the day of graduation, I paid the rental fee and picked up my cap and gown. I got 3¢ back in change. I had enough money for breakfast the next morning in the cafeteria, but that was it.

I was on my way to the graduation ceremony when I saw someone walking toward me. It was my nephew from Pittsburgh. Two carloads of relatives had shown up to see me graduate. I was so happy to see my mother and father and siblings there. One of the sisters who showed up was the one who had called me a fool so long ago when I told her that I had signed up for the army to get the GI Bill for college.

After the ceremony, I took my cap and gown back to the bookstore, turned it in, and rode home with my family. I was happy because I had a ride home, and I would not have to thumb a ride to get home to Dozier. I only had 3¢ to my name when I graduated.

A few weeks later, we began to pick cotton, and I earned enough to pay Tuskegee the $50 I borrowed for graduation fees. Although I had the GI Bill, the funds had run out during the last month of the summer session.

In December, I received my orders to enter the army in February of 1960. After I finished helping my family with the cotton, I got a job at a sawmill owned by Mr. Corner Faison. Out of all the mill owners, he was the most honest. He paid your Social Security taxes, and he gave you a copy of your earning for your records so you could pay your income taxes. He and the president of the bank in Dozier were truly outstanding men of character and goodwill.

I worked for Mr. Faison until it was time to report for duty at my first duty station at Fort Benjamin Harrison in Indiana. I arrived four days before I was to report and took a train ride to Dayton, Ohio, to visit some friends I took there in 1955.

Even after reporting for duty, I continued to study. If I went out with the guys on Saturday night, I spent Sunday in the library studying. During the second week, after studying all day Sunday, I decided to take a break and get something to eat.

On the way to eat, I was approached by two young ladies needing direction to catch a bus to town. I didn't have a car, but there was an acquaintance of mine who had one. He was a lieutenant who had graduated from Tuskegee in 1956.

He agreed to take the young ladies home. We took them to dinner and then home, but not before I got the telephone number of the young lady with pretty teeth. I told her that if I had time, I would take her out. The other young lady noticed an officer's sticker on the lieutenant's car and told my young lady that they should hold on to us because we were officers.

I enjoyed meeting the young lady from Indiana and further enjoyed her company very much. I met her mother first, then her father and some of her brothers. But my work in the army was my priority. I ceased dating for a while, but I missed her.

The next time I saw her, I spoke with her mother and told her how I felt about her daughter. I wanted her very much but didn't have the time to pursue her because my goal was to complete my training successfully.

I wanted to finish at or near the top of my class and was on the way to reaching that goal when I came down with a major toothache just before our second test. The tooth extraction kept me out of class for three days and caused my grades and my class standing to drop.

I received orders for Fort Ord, California, but the last week of training, my orders were changed to Barstow, California.

The week before my graduation in 1960, I gave my young lady an engagement ring, and we planned the wedding for the following June in California. I got engaged to my spouse in Indiana at the conclusion of my basic officers course at Fort Benjamin Harrison in Indiana. We planned our wedding in California for June 1961. My spouse had a young lady who worked with her at the hospital in Indiana. They became friends. She moved to California and met a young man. This was ideal that she was her maid of honor. Three other young ladies that attended college with me were stationed at the base hospital in Riverside, California, located at March Air Force Base. They all participated in our wedding. The best man was a captain in the medical service corps. He left the army and returned to medical school.

Wedding Ceremony

Looking back over the years, the wedding was a great occasion. We had a packed house for the wedding and the reception. At the base, they had a great tradition that allowed my new wife and I to ride to the wedding reception in a tank. This was a tradition that started back in the '40s.

The second tradition they had on base was for the newlyweds to spend two days in Las Vegas. We could not go to Vegas because we were black. The town was off the list. We instead went to March Air Force Base for a few days.

I purchased a 1956 Pontiac car in 1960. We had dinner, and the next morning, I left to drive to Alabama. I had some property to get rid of; I had a logging business. My brother was supposed to lease the truck out to a relative, but I never saw any of the proceeds if he did. The truck was broken down. I had to have it fixed soon or salvaged.

My youngest sister was very happy to see me when I returned to Dozier because she needed someone to take her and her friend to the senior banquet at her school in Luverne. I put on my summer dress uniform and was escorting them through the line when the principal saw me and shouted that he couldn't believe his eyes. He kept saying, "I don't believe what I'm seeing. I don't believe what I'm seeing."

This was the same principal who told me that I wasn't college material when I wanted him to send my transcript to Tuskegee. I am probably the first person from that Luverne school to complete college and earn a commission. After that meeting, I don't think I ever saw that principal again.

I went home and got rid of the property, a truck and some saws. I then purchased insurance for the car and returned to Indiana. On the way back, I caught a very bad cold. When I arrived in Indiana, I spent two days with my fiancée's family before we left for California. We, and a cousin from my father's side who was running from the law, departed on a Sunday evening and arrived in Barstow that Wednesday.

My cousin had been in trouble for stealing. When I took him to Indiana, I didn't know the extent of his troubles. I got lodging on the base, where we spent two days. That Saturday evening, we went out with the gorgeous lady from Indiana to a nightclub. On the third day, we left for California. I picked the young man up because of his grandmother; she had given me a few dollars to assist with expenses. It wasn't enough, but I accepted it to make her happy. He was out of jail. I took him to California to keep him out of more trouble or a long prison sentence.

I drove to Camp Irwin after I dropped my cousin off in Barstow. From there, I went was thirty-seven miles across the desert. When I got there, I went straight to the hospital and was admitted immediately. I was very sick; I had almost caught pneumonia.

I heard that my cousin turned his life around and became a model citizen. Much later, I visited the Sixth Army headquarters in the presidio, where we had dinner, and then I returned to Barstow. The next day, this young man became a model citizen.

Military Assignments

I served on active duty in the army from February of 1960 until September of 1973 when reduction in personnel caused my separation. I served as personnel officer and assistant adjutant general at the Barstow, California, military base in Southern California.

My main duty was to handle all personnel operations for the base. During the Berlin Crisis, I processed a battalion from Alabama in less than one week from the time they were activated and they entered active duty. We had a liaison officer from the Sixth U.S. Army who observed operations. He was impressed and told six army officials what I had done. I should have received the Legion of Merit for my efficiency, but I received nothing but shoddy evaluations from my superior later.

The job I did in Barstow in processing a battalion on duty from the reserve was nothing short of a miracle. In less than a week's time, troops came early, and we got them paid so they and their families could eat. Then we processed the entire battalion on duty. At the end of the month, everybody in the entire battalion was paid. The battalion came to the base in the middle of the week. My spouse was five months pregnant. I did not take or seek a deferment though I was entitled to one. I could have gotten a deferment, but I didn't because I could not stand this evil man. The rater had a hatred for blacks, and he did everything he could to damage their reputation. He gave me the lowest rating possible for all my work. Many of my military accomplishments will remain unknown and unacknowledged.

The entire command structure knew the captain that evaluated me was not qualified and was incompetent. During the Berlin buildup, if a top secret message came over the wire, they would get staff together to go over the message. My rater, who was the adjutant general of the base, could not open the safe even though he had the combination down. We were not supposed to have it in writing; this was secret, but he had written it down and still could not open the safe. The commander and all the staff knew that if I were called to come down and open the safe, I could, which happened every night. When I left the commander, only one senior officer came by to talk to me. He was a kind man who gave me the credit due for how well I had performed. The person who came by to see me was a G-3; we stood and talked between two buildings for an hour. He knew that I had been shafted by the AG, and he told me so. He told me it was impossible to do what I did in such a short period of time and have a record of accomplishment.

I wasn't required to go overseas because I was eligible for a deferment, but I went anyway. My superior hated blacks from the bottom of his heart. He had entered the army in the tenth grade, took the test for his GED, applied for OCS, and got a commission. This man had written a recommendation to deny extension of a service obligation for another African American officer. Likewise, I was denied. My superior, however, was exonerated.

I served in Vietnam and got no credit for the job I did there, either. Other guys who served with me came home with ribbons on their chests. Yet you couldn't find them when it was time for their duty assignments on weekends. They could not be found.

I was always available because I did not have any money. My spouse had to live with her parents on her $300-per-month allotment while my pay was $47 per month. I was barely able to exist for the one year I was in Vietnam. Halfway to completing my term in Vietnam, I was able to earn supplemental income by securing a part-time position at a school near the base. I taught English to the Vietnamese who wanted to work for the army. This is how I was able to send a few items back home to my spouse. One day while in the dining facility, one of my comrades, Earl Woods, Tiger Woods's father, notified me that my daughter was born. I was very happy to return to the States. Our daughter was nine months old when I returned. I could not keep my hands off her. I was so happy to see my wife after a year in Vietnam.

I returned to my permanent unit after I completed my first tour in Vietnam. It was the HQ of the Thirty-fifth Artillery Brigade at Fort Meade, Maryland. My assignment required me to take a course on recruiting. I was sent back to Fort Benjamin Harrison in Indiana, where all the members in the office of the adjutant general had medals on their chest. One even had a Bronze Star. This really took me back. I had done all the work, but as usual, they had gotten rewarded and were able to stand proudly, showing off their medals. This upset me so much that I wanted to leave active duty.

In the meantime, my wife had met another army wife who talked about how much she and her husband enjoyed being stationed in Europe. My wife was convinced that we should do a tour in Europe before I left the service. At that time, our daughter was three, and our new son was born in the hospital in Indiana. Since there was really nothing meaningful to do where I was stationed, I used my little influence at the Pentagon and was transferred to the personnel office of the second recruiting district. I had turned this unit around but never got credit for it; instead, I was sent to Baltimore because my immediate rating officer was displeased by the overseas assignment I had received upon completion of the officers advanced course in Fort Harrison, Indiana. My spouse left Maryland early to leave for Indiana in order to prepare for the birth of our son, George IV. He was born on the eighteenth of February 1965.

The commander came to see me before the letter was sent through channels to Washington. He told me about the letter. He said that he didn't agree with it, and in his heart, he couldn't send it. He told me to go ahead and make preparations for a change-of-command ceremony, where I could assume command of the station. He did tell me that he wouldn't be there because his staff wanted to deny me the command at the change-of-command ceremony. The expense for this ceremony depleted our unit's funds, but it was worth it. We invited the entire command, including all of the enlisted recruiters' spouses.

My immediate rating officer received a telegram from the Office of the Adjutant General on my new assignment. Even though I had done an outstanding job as the director of personnel, he saw my new assignment as moving ahead of him. The rating officer had never been to the Adjutant General School, and seeing me go there was too much for him to take. I was to be sent to Baltimore when the outgoing commander was to be transferred. He went after me again by writing me up, stating that I was unfit to command the Baltimore station as the new commander. This is the reason the commander came to see me and show me the letter before it was sent through channels to Washington. I don't know how this officer was commissioned. He had no formal schooling at the branch school in Fort Benjamin Harrison, Indiana, at that time.

I was shipped to the Baltimore, Maryland, recruiting station as the adjutant. The commander received orders for overseas two months later. I was next in line to assume his command after he left. Unfortunately, my rating officer convinced the commander that I was unfit to command, and he prepared a letter to Washington denying me the opportunity.

At the change-of-command ceremony, the outgoing commander spoke first; then, it was my turn. I had no notes, so I just looked out over the crowd and a thought came to me and I began to speak. I talked to each recruiter and his spouse. I told them that we had gone too long without meeting our recruitment goals and that we were letting our commands down. We had been three years without meeting our quota, three years.

The executive officer of the district, after meeting with me at a function at the commander's home, told me that I was in the wrong branch of service. So I assumed command of a unit that had failed to meet its recruiting objective for three years. The very first month of command, I met our quota. How did I do this? I went out to visit every recruiter, looked at their plans, and made recommendations. My input was effective, and for the three months I was in command of the Baltimore recruiting main station, we were at the very top. The executive officer told me to throw away my adjutant general brass and get one for combat arms because that was where I belonged. He thought I had clearly demonstrated that I was a leader. He went so far as to compare my leadership skills to General Patton of World War II fame.

Then I spoke to the wives. I told them that they were just as much a part of this letdown as their husbands. I talked about how a wife needs to motivate her husband to do his best. I told them that they were part of a team and that they were in this race until the end. Then I gave out a list of prizes that the top fifteen recruiters and their wives would receive at the end of the month, every month. We had a system to get prizes from two organizations to give each recruiter's spouse, as well as a prize for each person recruited, for the top fifteen recruiters.

The first month, we met our quota of recruits for the first time in three years. I received a call from the station commander in Philadelphia, who laughed and said, "Even a blind hog will find an acorn now and then."

The next month, our numbers were even higher. Calls began to come in from the Pentagon. They wanted to know the name of my female recruiter. I told them we didn't have one but that we had two young ladies who were very active with soldier activities—one worked for the company that makes Seagram's Seven and the other for Woodruff and Lathrop. I gave them the name of a very overweight male recruiter. They couldn't believe it. The Pentagon sent an LTC up to see the female recruiter and was really surprised to find that we had none. The secretary at Seagram's Seven and the young lady from Woodruff were active with the military. One was Miss USA. Their jobs gave them a chance to help the wives of the soldiers. Wives were not making much money at that time. They were happy to be in line to get the $75 gift certificate from Woodruff and Lathrop.

As time went on, calls began to come in from recruiting stations all over the country. I even received a call from the recruiter who had taught the course on recruiting in Indiana, at Fort Benjamin Harrison.

He wanted to know what I was doing to move a station after three years as the commander. Prior to my arrival, for three years, the quota was not met. Once I arrived, within the first month, we met our quota after years of not making our goals.

I completed my AG advanced courses and then left for Stuttgart, Germany. After spending ninety days as the assistant staff postal officer in the Seventh Army, I was promoted to staff postal officer of the Seventh Army. The officer that was supposed to sign my officer evaluation form said he did not know me, so my record would be blank for my first one-hundred-day evaluation period. We worked in the same section, but he wanted the position and would not rate me, my endorsing officer.

At that time, the Seventh Army was the largest field army in the world, so you can imagine that the problems we had were numerous. The personnel did not know how to handle and treat the mail, and a number of soldiers had been put in positions for which they had no training.

I wrote a paper with recommendations regarding these problems to the adjutant general of the Seventh Army. My suggestions were approved, and funds were allotted for me to conduct several two-week training courses in postal operations for four divisions and nine army postal units (APU). Each division sent two men to the classes, and the army postal units sent eighteen. We had a total of twenty-six students in each class.

I would leave Stuttgart, Germany, early in the morning on Monday during postal inspections and return every other Thursday to award diplomas and speak to the graduating class. I even gave a speech before diplomas were awarded. The program concluded when all the clerks who had handled mail had been trained. I had wrapping paper installed at each post office. The personnel became very proficient. This also helped customers. They learned how to wrap the package we accepted for mailing. This really made the post office look professional with the work the troopers did.

I took the E-7 from my office and the NCO from the thirtieth APU in Stuttgart, Germany. I ordered training material from Fort Benjamin Harrison in Indiana. But I also made sure I was there at the graduation at the end of the two weeks, and usually, I gave the speech and passed out the diplomas.

The courses were very successful. Before, the number of mail claims was over 1,400 each quarter in the command, Seventh Army. By the time my tour was over, the number had dropped to 200 fewer claims per quarter. Before I left, the general sent for me. He wanted to tell me personally what a great job I had done. He told me that it would be very hard to find someone to replace me. He reviewed my performance and what I had done. He wanted to thank me personally. What I did as a captain was truly remarkable. I held down a job that required a staff of seven people with only myself and an enlisted for thirty months. In my last year of this assignment, I got a senior NCO.

He was right about replacing me. A sergeant kept me up to date about my replacements until he rotated back to the States. He said they were on their third replacement when he left them. I should have gotten a Legion of Merit because I filled a slot for an LTC chief of the branch. A major and a captain received the Army Commendation Medal, which I had to ask for and write up the recommendation myself. My recommendation was downgraded from the Legion of Merit to an Army Commendation Medal.

Memories of My Mother

There was an instructor at Dozier High School who was an expert in cabinetmaking. My mother learned about his trade by looking at cabinets he had made for many whites in the area. She kept mentioning his work to my father, but he never gave her the funds to make a purchase—especially since the cedar chest she wanted cost $30. I told her that I would get it for her as soon as I received my first check from the army. I kept my word. When I got my first check, I sent it to her, and she bought the cedar chest. The chest is still with us at the home in Dozier. My mother marveled at this piece of furniture all her life. She used it to store quilts and documents with the top shelves in back being reserved for important documents. I think that the cabinet and my graduation from Tuskegee in four years are two of the greatest memories of her life.

I remember that my mother washed clothes twice a week when I was young: every Monday and Thursday. She had to wash because we only had two sets of clothes. We didn't wear underwear except in the winter, and then you only had two sets of underwear. When spring came, you had to remove your underwear and pass them on to your younger brothers.

There was a farmer in Covington County who owned a very large tobacco plantation. He would pick us up every morning during the summer to help pick the tobacco crops. After we shared our earnings with our mother, we ordered clothes from Sears and Roebuck in Atlanta. When we wrote up our order, we included underwear. So from the ninth grade until I finished high school, I had underwear during the summer months.

My eldest brother dropped out of high school in the eighth grade, and the next eldest stopped in the tenth grade. The eldest one did end up in the U.S. Air Force. He trained to be a mechanic and was an excellent soldier who was highly regarded and the recipient of numerous awards and achievement medals.

I once asked him why he stayed in the air force. He told me that he always wanted to be a pilot. He had gone to Florida and completed training to become a pilot, but he never returned to military service after that. He did not have the education needed to enter the air force as an air force pilot. He should have gone to school and prepared himself. He had the GI Bill but refused to use it. I hated to see this opportunity go to waste.

The younger brother, Lester Lee, was in the quartermaster corps. He also served well. When his term was over, he visited a young lady at Alabama State University, whom he had dated before he entered military service. He came home after one visit to see her and fell on his knees and prayed. He did this for several weeks and then he stopped. I couldn't understand why he was doing it at first. The young lady had told him that the romance was over and that he was free to see another partner or find someone else.

I finally found out that his young lady had found a new fellow—a student at Alabama State. He also had served in the army—in his case, as a lieutenant in the Ninety-Second Infantry Division in Europe during World War II. This young fellow hailed from Searight, near Dozier, and was the only black commissioned officer from Crenshaw in World War II.

My brother prayed, but the Lord never answered his prayers. The young lady married the former lieutenant, and they both ended up teaching in Georgia for more than thirty-five years. This just reinforced my dedication to study hard at night. I often would think about my brother and his long prayers at night. He was married in 1948 to someone else, and they were married for almost sixty years before he died.

Although both of my brothers had the GI Bill for education, neither of them took advantage of it. They made excuses that they would go if all of the newly separated soldiers would go to school together. My younger brother had written to this barber school in Texas, and the plan was that a group of them would attend school there. But he and the other ex-soldiers never went.

I could not understand how they could pass up this opportunity. Of all the soldiers I knew in the war, two became career servicemen, and only four of them went to school. One attended Alabama State, two went to Tuskegee, and another to New York to medical school, I heard. We lost contact with him in late 1956, so I don't know if he actually went to medical school. I do know that he was in New York and this was his goal.

In the fall of 1949, we moved to another farm as our former landlord wanted to use the land for grazing and raising cattle. We had lived on the Sports plantation for ten years. This is the plantation where I learned to plow in the fifth grade. When I reached sixteen years of age, we finally had our own mules to plow. I started plowing at the age of eleven, when I was in the fifth grade. At sixteen, I was very happy to plow with a mule we owned. The land was much better, and we planted over 120 acres.

We picked twenty-five to thirty bales of cotton each year. I was extremely happy because for the first time since I was in the fifth grade, we owned our own mules. The contract between the owner and my family changed: we were now getting three bales to one bale for the owner of the plantation.

My father purchased two mules from a relative who had decided not to farm anymore. This relative decided to go to work for a mill owner. He had an accident in the summer of 1953 while I was overseas. He was killed when a tree fell on him.

Later that year, his son, my cousin Charlie, was discharged from the army because he had diabetes. His mother passed away ten years later. He moved his family to Tuskegee and began training to become an x-ray technician with the Veterans Administration Hospital. We remained close until he passed away in 1974. I was the best man at his wedding in 1959.

My mother was very ingenious during the winter months. She made most of our clothes and belonged to a group of ladies who took turns hosting quilting parties. I remember that the quilt patterns they used had names like rattlesnake or fish hook or turkey trot. The quilts were kept in a very large closet.

A major storm came through Dozier, and my parents had to have their carpet replaced. The necessary work was done, but the workers stole all the quilts while working. That broke my mother's heart and angered my father, and it led to the beginning of their locking the house and the smokehouse. We had never had anyone break into the house or steal from us before.

I visited my mother long after the incident, in early 1976, and she was still upset by what had happened. I was visiting to help celebrate the 125th anniversary of the church built by the freed slaves. She was trying to replace the quilts, but she never got the opportunity to finish. She became ill and spent her last two months in the hospital before she passed away in 1983.

It is entirely possible to me that her heartache over the loss of so many cherished quilts hastened her death. Yet although we didn't get the number of quilts we all expected, I am pleased with what I have. Had the quilts not been stolen, each family member would have received ten quilts.

I will trust in the Lord, I will trust in the Lord, I will trust in the Lord until I die.

Till I die, I will trust in the Lord, I will trust in the Lord, I will trust in the Lord until I die.

This was a favorite hymn my mother would sing, usually while preparing breakfast and dinner. When things didn't seem to be going right, she would start singing, and this was one of the many songs she would sing. When we heard her singing, you knew something was on her mind, and it worried her. I remember her singing this hymn to the man who had wanted me to marry his daughter when I was in college.

May 28

On May 28 of every year, as far back as I can remember, we would all gather at the river for a celebration. As I got older, I wanted to understand exactly what it was we were celebrating. I learned during Black History Week that it was the date that people in our area got word that the slaves were freed. This was a great celebration that required a great deal of preparation.

The men would leave in one or two wagons to begin fishing only in the morning. If our grandfather went fishing with them, we would prepare for a lot of fish. He was the greatest catcher of fish that I ever knew. When he attended the celebration, we know we would have plenty of fish. Many times he would go to the river, and if he was not back by about five or six o'clock, we would hitch up the wagon to go meet him at the river and load up the fish he had caught.

The ladies would join the men around noon to start preparing to cook because by then the fish would be caught and cleaned. Around one or two o'clock, the fish fry would start.

Observance of the date set aside to celebrate the slaves' freedom slowly ended before I finished high school. It was a shame because that was a great communal occasion, and I often think about it. Of all the celebrations like reunions and birthday, this had the greatest meaning because it represented the freeing of a whole group of people who had been slaves, including my great-grandfather.

Return from Overseas

In June 1968, I returned to the United States and was assigned as the chief of the mail distribution and postal branch, Office of the Adjutant

General (AG), First U.S. Army. When I was chief of this branch, I solved three major tasks for the army, plus other functions.

We sent several reserve army postal units to Vietnam. When they arrived in the country, they could not do their jobs. I was not involved in the process to evaluate their unit before they left for Vietnam. They were sent before I got to Fort Meade. A letter came through the channel commander and ended up on my desk from the commander in Vietnam. I saw the problem and went to the Department of Defense to get fixed credits. They trained clerks on postal operations and other postal services. We opened up a post office for them to train soldiers at their bases. They became proficient. I went out on an inspection tour to visit the units in action. I went back and told the AG that these units were ready for deployment. They went, and every unit that came from First Army hit the ground running. During this period, we had a postal strike. I set up a system for all official mail for all units in the First Army to be delivered in designated pickup points and to be picked up to carry back to their bases. This went on until the strike was over.

On March 28, 1969, our second son was born. We were extremely happy because we had space in our three-bedroom apartment for our daughter and two sons.

When the Office of the Adjutant General received replacements, they were given to other branches. A sergeant major told me on one occasion that the men coming out of AIT would fit my setup. I never got any new recruits. I had to interview men who were in the stockade to get help in operating the mail and distribution division. In this process, I ended up turning around a lot of men who were destined for trouble. So many lives were effectively changed that they wanted to give me an award. The men who handled mail during the day worked on an exhibit in the evening. During the day, the men were exemplary. Each person from my office received commendations from the post commander. I thought of this as a crowning achievement during the two years I was in charge. When I returned to Vietnam for my second tour, we had a special celebration for the mail and distribution team.

For three years, the base had requested a post office to be built because the space for highly classified, top secret material was limited. The chief of the branch showed me the rejection of the project, which had been turned down three times. The project was very low on the priority list. Then the chief told me to get the job done. I was told that if I succeeded, I would receive a special officer evaluation report (OER). In other words, I would be walking on water. I accepted the challenge, and it was during this time that a picket ship was captured. The ship carried classified materials, and it went to the National Security Agency located at Fort George G. Meade, Maryland. The classified material was to be delivered to the National Security Agency (NSA).

I wrote up the order requesting a new post office, did a study, and it went through channels a second time to the DOD. They sent a team out to see the facility. After reading the report to justify why a new post office should be approved, they came back a second time. I had all the postmasters within thirty miles to come to a luncheon, including the deputy AG of the First Army. We were briefed on the status of the proposal. The post office was approved to be built. I never received the special OER (officer evaluation report) or, for that matter, any medal whatsoever. I wanted to leave the army, but our eldest son was involved in a major car accident in our neighborhood, so I stayed so he could receive over two years of surgery that he needed. Since I was not leaving the service, I was sent a second time to Vietnam. I never got the special officer evaluation report.

When I returned from Vietnam, my eldest son still had one more operation that he needed performed, and it was done at Indiana medical center in Indianapolis, Indiana. Because of this, I was given a compassion reassignment to remain in Indiana at the Fort Benjamin Harrison. My assignment was special project officer. I organized the first combined federal campaign for the base. The campaign was successful.

I spent the least amount of money and raised more than any other organization in the nation for a post that size.

In Vietnam, the first rating I received from an officer was on my second tour in Vietnam. The officer was a graduate of Texas A&M, who had taken our command from a previous commander of the advisory team at the Seventh Vietnamese Division. He was a very sharp individual. We had several discussions about my work as the G-1 advisory team leader. This person checked my record and was really upset by how I had been treated in most of my assignments. I left Vietnam with five medals: a Bronze Star, second oak-leaf cluster for the Army Commendation Medal, and three other Vietnamese awards. In reviewing my assignment, this was the first officer who rated me that had a college degree. He knew leadership, and it showed on my evaluation.

We began to have a lot of racial tension on the base at Fort Harrison. A report reached Washington regarding the likely place a similar action was likely to happen. They named five or six bases. Fort Harrison was on the list. I saw it coming. They changed my assignment, and I became the race relations officer. They dispatched a major to Fort Harrison. I studied the problem and made a report to the commander. He called a meeting of all the commanders to hear my report, including the major from Washington. I gave them five recommendations; each recommendation was explained, and they were approved. The bad apples were soldiers who had volunteered for individual training. They failed and were not reassigned away from Fort Harrison. The command agreed with me, and all these bad apples were reassigned elsewhere in the army. Some went overseas after returning in a new MOS (military occupational specialty) at new bases. The soldiers enlisted to receive AIT (advanced individual training). If they failed the training, the army had met its obligation. We used this to move these soldiers to other specialties out of Fort Harrison. The problem was solved. During this period, they began a reduction in force, and I was let out of the army as a major in the reserves.

I joined the U.S. Army Reserve immediately, with an assignment as a BOAC (basic officers advance course) instructor. After one year, I left and returned to the control group in St. Louis, Missouri. Why did I leave this unit? I left because at the annual training for AG officers advance course, I was voted the most outstanding instructor in the school. However, when my evaluation was given in October, it did not reflect what I had accomplished, so I walked away from this assignment. I found another unit and joined. Another unit was formed, and I joined as the executive officer of the 376th Personnel and Administrative Battalion. After one year, I became the commander of the 425th Personnel Service Company. I remained in this unit until I was transferred to Georgia in 1978. As the commander of the 425th, we did our camp at Fort Carson, Colorado. This was the first time the unit trained on a military post.

Move to Georgia

We had a very small program with a few historically black colleges and universities (HBCUs) in the region. In the spring of 1981, Washington held a conference with all the HBCUs in Jacksonville, Florida. This was right after the air traffic controller strike. All agencies that were invited to attend sent their presidents and the director of placement and/or cooperative education director. I represented the Southern Region. I was the last person to speak to the presidents on the second day. When I completed my presentation, the presidents lined up to see me. I took all their names. I reported the results to the FAA, Southern Region. Of all the HBCUs in the region, only one institution did not want to be a part of the coop program with the FAA.

Prior to reporting to the Southern Region, I was the manager of the Indianapolis Center in the Great Lakes region. From the first day I reported for duty in the Southern Region, I made my mark. I was a great motivator of young students in high school and in college. Morris Brown College was the first HBCU to join the coop program in the Southern

Region. We brought the coop director for the signing ceremony. The region was flooded with applicants from HBCUs.

Initially, we began testing at four sites in the Southern Region. After the initial testing, the office of personnel management developed a noncompetitive test for the air traffic coop program and a program for agencies who wanted to move to the air traffic occupation as air traffic control specialists. When the noncompetitive tests were developed, we began to schedule testing at all the HBCUs in the region. We would leave on a Monday and visit HBCUs in South Carolina then North Carolina. We would do this in one week to save funds. The second week, we would go to Knoxville, Tennessee State, and Fisk universities, spend the night, then proceed to LeMoyne-Owen College in Memphis. From there we would then travel to Mississippi Valley State University, Jackson State University, Tougaloo College, and then on to Alcorn State University. If it was Friday and the first weekend of the month, I had to make sure I was back in Atlanta to attend U.S. Army Reserve training. The next week, we would visit Talladega College, Miles College, Mississippi State, Stillman, Alabama State, Tuskegee, and Judson College. When you returned to the region, the tests were sent away for grading by the office of personnel management, and then you completed the paperwork. If funds were available, you visited the college in Florida. Of all of the HBCUs, South Carolina State and Jackson State always had a full house for the tests. Twice each year, after two work periods, the students graduated. We had a few who stayed for a third work session if they were selected as sophomores. We did have one student who did six work sessions. The six work periods had to be approved by the U.S. Department of Transportation. I went through the channels and was approved.

When our first class graduated and was sent to the academy in Oklahoma, we waited with bated breath until graduation. Each region sent teams to the FAA Academy to place successful graduates. Our initial class was approximately 65 percent of the coops that graduated. This required action by the personnel office to find a remedy. We raised the initial GPA and the test scores for those who were allowed to enter the coop program. Two years later, it began to pay off. Starting with graduates from the FAA Academy, it went up to above 85 percent of the graduation rates at the FAA Academy. These were coop students. The 85 percent was for all attendees at the academy. Sometimes these students achieved almost 100 percent of the graduation rate from the academy. When the change was made to raise the GPA and test scores, I was criticized by persons in the civil rights division, but the air traffic division supported me, and look at the results.

The air traffic coop program grew every year. At its highest point, we had well over three hundred students in the program. There are students from Tougaloo College, New York, Virginia, New Jersey, and California. When these students completed the FAA Academy in Oklahoma, they were assigned by their region to these locations.

I recall a statement by one of the attendees at the conference of HBCUs in Jacksonville, Florida, saying that if it can be done, the HBCUs would have a part of it. This person is no longer with us, but what he said was true—he was the president of Alcorn State University. What this president of this HBCU said at our initial conference has really assisted the agency in filling its ranks of qualified air traffic controller specialists from historically black colleges and universities.

Not only did the employees of the FAA benefit, but we also learned a lot of lessons from these applicants for the ATCS coop program. After the first work period for the initial class, they were evaluated by the supervisors. One young lady from Jackson State University came to me to complain about how she had been evaluated. I read the report and agreed with it. During our talk, I told her "You are lucky they could have let you go. They didn't, so you have a new chance to improve." I instructed her to take her evaluation to the dean of the English Department at Jackson State University and let him read it. Then to ask him if he can help her improve. She returned for her second work period and was amazed at her new evaluation. She graduated and was sent to the FAA Academy in Oklahoma City. She finished the academy successfully and was assigned to the tower in Jackson, Mississippi. She became certified but wanted to leave Jackson. At that time, there were vacancies in San Juan, Puerto Rico. She bid on it and was accepted. After she had become certified, she began to work at her position at ATCT. Later that week, a plane entered her airspace, and she gave him landing instructions. The pilot was intrigued by her voice and said he wanted to meet her. They eventually met and got to know each other. They have been married for more than twenty years and still live in Puerto Rico.

The experience I gained for operating the air traffic control coop program could fill several books. I recall another young man in the coop program who went home to visit his dying father. The father told him to finish school and assist his brothers and sisters. He returned to school to withdraw and move to Memphis and, in the process, try to find a job. He packed his clothes and went to withdraw from school, then he saw a letter on the wall that stated if a student took a full load and made straight As, they would be entitled to a scholarship to pay all their fees. He had the note and letter verified. He made up his mind to make straight As. That's how he remained in school. We let him in the coop program for ATCS. He completed the program and was offered employment as an air traffic control specialist trainee in Oklahoma City at the FAA Academy. He called me before he turned the offer down to tell me that he had an offer to get his masters and a PhD. I talked to this young man, and he went with my blessings.

For the twelve years we had the coop program in air traffic control, it was not because employees liked it. There were some in the FAA who didn't like the program at all. This was shown on the evaluation they gave the coop students. We had a case in Atlanta where a student was removed from the program. He returned to his college, and the president of the college called me through his director of cooperative education. After our conversation, I told the director of cooperative education that I would call him back in an hour. I called him back with a letter I had prepared for the president to sign to the regional administrator. A person not in the chain of command wrote that letter, and it was in error. It was rescinded, and the student was put back in the coop program and returned for another assignment. He completed his last assignment and was offered a position as an air traffic control trainee then went to the FAA Academy and came out first in his class. This young man made supervisor at the Jacksonville Air Route Traffic Control Center in Jacksonville, Florida, in record time.

Federal Employee Who Introduced Aviation at Historically Black Colleges and Universities Makes Quiet Exit

On October 1, 1995, a little-known federal employee in the Southern Region of the Federal Aviation Administration (FAA) retired. Although his exit was not revealed until the close of business the day prior to his departure, he left behind a legacy of accomplishments that will in all probability never be equaled. From September 1979 to January 1991, George W. Burnette III introduced cooperative education programs in aviation in 80 percent of the historically black colleges and universities in the Southeast. Over this period, well over eight thousand students, by taking the test, participated in cooperative education programs in the four regions of the FAA in air traffic control, engineering and electronic technology. During a five-year stretch of this period, he never used air transportation, instead electing to drive to reach as many students as possible on the meager travel budget allocated to support the program. His reason for not announcing his retirement and scheduling a luncheon or dinner was because hundreds of former program participants would have come or spent funds for gifts. He would rather have them contribute the money they would have spent for such an event to their college or university for scholarships.

Fiftieth Anniversary April 3-5, 2009

I returned to Tuskegee on the first Sunday in April. It was the fiftieth anniversary of my class. I sat there and recalled all the classes I took and many of the classmates. I thought how sharp many of the students were. Then I would think about myself. We had members of my class who would actually draw pictures of the instructor and take the test and make straight As. All these thoughts went through my mind as I observed many of the activities at the celebrations.

After completing one year at Tuskegee, I was placed on probation. I registered for my second year and got the news from the registrar. I had to reduce the number of hours I could take. Not only did I have to reduce my number of hours, but I also had to begin going to school year round to repeat courses I had taken and did not have a C average. I took English and math three times—history twice.

Monday morning breakfast—corn muffins and syrup. A lot of ladies did not like this breakfast. I did. This was one of the few days I liked to sit with the ladies because the ladies did not like corn fritters and syrup. I would trade my bacon for these corn fritters.

About the Author

Colonel George W. Burnette III (ret. U.S. Army) did a tour at the infantry center at Fort Benning, Georgia, at the Pentagon in the Office of the Adjutant General, publication branch, and also completed three different assignments as a member of a selections board for lieutenant colonels, majors, and captains at the U.S. Army personnel center in St. Louis, Mississippi, and also served as the adjutant general of the Eighty-first U.S. Army Reserve Command in East Point, Georgia, and as chief of operations and readiness division, HQ of the Third U.S. Army at Fort McPherson, Georgia, for four years.

He was selected to be the adjutant general of the Eighty-first U.S. Army Reserve Command after three other officers turned it down. They all quit after one drill. He was called and given the assignment. He accepted the assignment because he had a history of turning units around. This unit had failed three consecutive AIG inspections by the First U.S. Army. They had less than one hundred days to get ready. They passed the AIG inspection. Burnette retired from the active reserve in November 1989.

In retirement, Burnette does volunteer work at Hillside Presbyterian Church, preparing a weekly luncheon for seniors. He also serves as an elder of the session. In addition to his local service, he serves as a member of the Presbyterian Council for Chaplains and Military Personnel in Washington DC (his recent duty at a council meeting was extended four days by the blizzard of '96).

CIVILIAN AWARDS

FAA – Administrator Award for Excellence in EEO 1996

The Anderson Award – National Black Federal Aviation, National Black Administration Award 2008

National Black Coalition Award – memorial dinner 2008

Certificate of Achievement – Outstanding Performance Appraisal for 1983, 1985, 1986, 1988, 1990

Cash Awards – 1982, 1988, 1991

Quality within-grade increase – 1983

Twenty letters of commendation

Military Awards

Bronze Service Medal
Meritorious Service Medal, second oak-leaf cluster
Army Commendation Medal, first oak-leaf cluster
Staff Service Medal, Army of Vietnam
Honor Medal First Class, Army of Vietnam
Army of Occupation Medal
Good Conduct Medal
European Theater Operations Medal
ACM Germany
National Defense Medal
AFRM Medal
AERM Medal
ROUNCM Medal 1960
USM Medal
Four overseas bars

Formal Education

Tuskegee University BS 1959 Commissioned 2nd Lieutenant August 14,
    1959
George Washington University 1963–67
Boston University 1965–67
University of Baltimore School of Law 1968–70
Butler University 1973
Indiana University 1977–78
Georgia State University 1980

Military Promotions

First lieutenant August 27, 1961
Captain December 9, 1963
Major August 1971
Lieutenant colonel November 1979
Colonel November 1984

Military Education

Adjutant General Basic Officers Course 1960
Adjutant General Officers Advance Course 1965
U.S. Army Command and General Staff College 1978
National Defense University (ICAF) 1980–81
National Security Seminar 1980–85

Work Experience

Extensive military service, active and reserve for more than thirty years, serving in grades from private to colonel in military command and staff assignments in personnel operation, plans, administration, postal operations, and combat advisory services to a foreign army from division, installation to theater field army level and joint staff in unified commands in the United States, the Far East, Europe, the Middle East, Africa, and the Pentagon. Served two tours in Vietnam. Retired in November 16, 1989.

Private Sector/Government Employment

Registered representative, IDS
Personnel manager, Indianapolis Center

Acting manager, Special Emphasis Program Staff, FAA Southern Region

Regional recruiting coordinator, FAA Southern Region

Manager, airway science, aviation education, college relations and cooperative education, Southern Region FAA.

Retired from FAA October 1, 1995

Member, Hillside Presbyterian Church since 1980

Founding and charter member of the 100 Black Men of America, Dekalb County Chapter

Member, Presbyterian Council for Chaplains and Military Personnel

Elder, Hillside Presbyterian Church (served two terms on session)

Hobbies

Married Bertha A. (Craig) on June 23, 1961, in Barstow (Camp Irwin), California

Three adult children: Melanie R., George W. IV, and Todd C.

Seven grandchildren: Toussaint, Alexandria, Cody, Savannah, George W. V, and twins Zachary and Zoe

Brief Biographical Summary

George Washington Burnette III

Born during the Depression in rural Crenshaw County, Alabama, the seventh of eleven children born to the union of Arvester and Georgia Lee Burnette, conservative Southern Missionary Baptists.

The family has had one or more members of the membership rolls of Springhill Missionary Baptist Church in Dozier, Alabama, since its founding in October 1877. Two brothers are presently deacons in the church, representing more than fifty years of continuous membership of a member of the family serving in that capacity. I attended Springhill during my youth but never joined.

The first six years of school was in a one-room building out in the woods, which also served as the home of Macedonia Missionary Baptist Church, which I joined in July 1946. We walked four miles each day to the school when we were able to go. I attended high school in Dozier until 1950 when it was converted to a junior high school. I completed the last two years of high school at Crenshaw County Training School in Luverne, Alabama, eighteen miles away. I received my high school diploma in May 1952, the first male member on either side of my family to do so.

I was called a fool when I joined the U.S. Army during the Korean War in October 1952 to get the GI Bill to attend college. I missed Korea, which is a story in itself, and served in Europe for eighteen months and was released from active duty as a corporal.

I had overall program implementation and responsibility for college and university relations in the Southern Region for the Federal

Aviation Administration. Responsible for graduate and undergraduate recruitment of applicants for direct hire as engineers and direct hire for other occupations where special authority is granted. Responsible for direct hire of airway science program graduates in five bachelor degree programs. Organized, planned, and coordinated the efforts of a staff to recruit and qualify over 150 college and university applicants annually for agencies through cooperative education programs in air traffic control, engineering, and electronic technology. Regional recruiting coordinator responsible for preparing a multiyear regional plan and coordinating the efforts of staff to ensure that sufficient applicants are recruited, examined, and qualified to meet regional staffing requirements for the air traffic control specialist occupation and other safety-related occupations. Traveled regionwide to conduct seminars on the airway science and cooperative education programs for the agency at participating colleges and universities. Delivered an average of fifty presentations annually to college and university student groups and organizations. Coordinated regional recruiting activity for collateral duty recruiters at career fairs and seminars at colleges and universities. Maintained certificates of eligibility for hiring in all airway science occupations.

From: Paquita Bradley, NBCFAE – ATL Chapter President
To: George Burnette
Sub: Re: George w. Burnette III honored in Charlotte at the NBCFAE (National
Black Coalition of Federal Aviation Employees Southern Region)
Date: Wed, 16 April 2008

Mr. Burnette was responsible for recruiting and hiring many African Americans and other minorities into the Federal Aviation Administration (FAA) during his appointment as Personnel Staffing Specialist in the Human Resource Management, Recruitment Branch in the Southern Region. Because of his hard work, dedication, and recruitment efforts, the Southern Region NBCFAE will be honoring him at our Regional Conference in Charlotte NC on May 8, 2008. The program will be at 11am in the Billy Graham Holiday Inn Hotel. Because of Mr. Burnette's talent, I was hired in 1981 as a GS-3 and have advance to the GS-14 level. I am actually a supervisor at the Atlanta Center in Hampton GA. We could never thank Mr. Burnette enough or put a price tag on what he did to help many of us young black children enter the field of aviation. One word I can use to describe (him) is UNFORGETTABLE, then there is AMAZING, and finally DEDICATED to helping those in need. Mr. Burnette travelled to Historically Black Colleges and Universities (HBCU's) and explain(ed) to us what the FAA had to offer and he made sure we did what was necessary to get into the workforce. This and many other reasons, is what our honoring him is all about. We want to let him know that we haven't forgotten his tireless journey and we as an organization are trying to walk in his footsteps. Now we don't have the hiring power like he did but we have the ability to go out and educate the children of the world today about the FAA and the many jobs the agency has to offer

■■■

WHY THIS BOOK

The purpose of this short book is to outline the steps one must take when you're fighting against all odds. My illnesses are almost too numerous to mention. I have had prostate surgery, tonsils removed, three heart attacks and a defibrillator, and a major stroke and diabetes. These are the major illnesses I have had. I will not mention the minor illnesses I have had to contend with.

Early in my life, I remember plowing my blind uncle's land; he could plant his crops on the land and make a living. As I worked the land, I would always think about my great-grandfather and wonder how he purchased a farm after slavery. He possessed a desire to move ahead in his life and that of his family. Each time I plowed the land, his son's, my thoughts would go back to my great-grandfather. This gave me courage to move ahead. The thought of my great-grandfather would enter my mind even as I tried to sleep at night after working the fields on the land that our great-grandfather purchased after slavery.

Many times, I wanted to give up, but the thought of my great-grandfather kept me moving until I finished high school—from the fifth grade until I finished high school, which was a miracle. I was in the twelfth grade and was about to be expelled. I spoke out with some other good students about why we were being expelled, and it was because some of the boys went off campus and purchased some moonshine. I asked the principal to smell my breath, to see if I had been drinking. Several other good students supported me, and we were not expelled. We had to be perfect until we graduated in May 1952.

This book is in memory of my great-grandfather—George W. Burnette Sr.

George W. Burnette singing a Sacred Harp song at Big Creek
Primitive Baptist Church in Alpharetta, Georgia, in 2010

SCHOOL DAYS

George W. Burnette senior high school, 1952

George W. Burnette, a young private in the U.S. Army in
Europe, 1953

George W. Burnette at a service club in Germany, U.S. Army

A November birthday celebration in Germany in 1954

My great-great grandfather began making syrup after
slavery on his farm. This is a picture of my father making
syrup in the backwoods of his house, 1978.

Graduating senior from Tuskegee University, 1959

U.S. Army Officer Basic Course for Second Lieutenant, 1960

An engagement present to my spouse, 1960

An engagement picture of my wife, 1960

Our wedding day in 1961 in Barstow, California

George W. Burnette riding a tank to the reception with his
new wife in 1961

George and Beth Burnette wedding reception on June 23, 1961

George W. Burnette on his second tour, U.S. Army, in Vietnam

Burnette family reunion in Luverne, Alabama, in 1972

Burnette family reunion in Andalusia, Alabama, in 1991

Burnette reunion in Andalusia, Alabama, in 1991

Burnette reunion in 1991

George W. Burnette is promoted to full colonel in the U.S. Army in 1984

George Burnette and his wife celebrating his promotion to a full colonel, 1984

Colonel George W. Burnette, U.S. Army, in 1986

My three children
Melanie (graduated from college)
George IV (junior at Auburn University)
Todd (a freshman at Morehouse College)

George and Beth Burnette enjoying a cruise in 1990

George and Beth on a relaxing cruise in 1991

Morris Brown College signing of the coop agreement with
the Federal Aviation Administration in 1982

U.S. Department
of Transportation

**Federal Aviation
Administration**

Aug. 24, 1992

NOTE TO: Mr. George Burnette
Personnel Staffing Specialist
Human Resource Management Division

Thank you so much for participating in our fifth annual
Airway Science (AWS) National Symposium. I am forwarding
the enclosed picture as a memento of your participation.

I enjoyed working with you this year and look forward to
your continued involvement in AWS Curriculum Program
initiatives.

Sincerely,

Margaret L. Powell
Manager, Airway Science Curriculum Program

TEAM WORK

makes the

DREAM WORK

SOUTHERN REGION
ANNUAL TRAINING CONFERENCE

MAY 11-14, 2010
ROSEN CENTRE HOTEL
ORLANDO, FLORIDA

WWW.NBCFAESO.ORG

The Negro National Anthem

The **Negro National Anthem** (also titled as **"Lift Every Voice and Sing"**) was written by James Weldon Johnson and J. Rosamond Johnson in 1899 to celebrate Black pride.

Lift Every Voice and sing till earth and heaven ring
Ring with the harmonies of liberty
Let our rejoicing rise high as the listening skies
Let it resound loud as the rolling sea

Sing a song, full of the faith that the dark past has taught us
Sing a song, full of the hope that the present has brought us
Facing the rising sum of our new day begun
Let us march on till victory is won

Stony the road we trod, bitter the chastening rod
felt in the days when hope unborn had died
yet with a steady beat, have not our weary feet
come to the place for which our fathers sighed?

We have come, over a way that with tears has been watered,
We have come, treading out path through the blood of the slaughtered,
Out of the gloomy past, till now we stand at last,
Where the white gleam of our bright star is cast

GOD of our weary years, GOD of our silent tears
Thou Who has brought us thus far on the way
Thou Who hast by Thy might, led us into the light
Keep us for-ever in the path we pray

Lest our feet, stray from the places our GOD where we met thee
Lest our hearts, drunk with the wine of the world we forget Thee
Shadowed beneath thy hand, may we forever stand
TRUE TO OUR GOD, TRUE TO OUR NATIVE LAND

CITY OF ORLANDO

May 11, 2010

Greetings,

As Mayor of the City of Orlando, it is my pleasure to welcome you to the "City Beautiful" and to The National Black Coalition of Federal Aviation Employees (NBCFAE) annual training conference.

Orlando is a City on the rise.

I encourage those of you visiting Orlando to experience all the things that make Orlando one of the fastest growing, most business-friendly and quality of life-centered cities in the nation.

Underneath a skyline that has doubled in just the last five years, our dynamic, bustling Downtown is alive with fine dining, exciting night life, fabulous shopping, year-round outdoor activities, arts and culture, professional sports and abundant parks.

Our vibrant and diverse culture is evidenced by the many distinctive neighborhoods that dot our City. I invite you to walk our red brick, tree lined streets, visit our beautiful historic districts or our Downtown Arts District and take in Orlando's crown jewel, Lake Eola Park.

Again, welcome to Orlando! We are happy to have you here and hope you enjoy taking part in the wonderful experiences that can only be found here.

Best wishes for a productive conference and continued success. I hope you enjoy your time here and I hope you visit Orlando again soon.

Sincerely,

Buddy Dyer

Buddy Dyer

Mayor

Greetings from the National President

On behalf of the National Black Coalition of Federal Aviation Employees (NBCFAE), I extend warm greetings to all of you attending the NBCFAE Southern Region Annual Training Conference here in Orlando, Florida. This event provides a platform for our conference theme, **"Team Work Makes The Dream Work."** It focuses on our continuing commitment to reach for new heights in professionalism and provide a positive impact for the future.

The denial of fair and equal treatment of minorities and women employees continues to be an issue in the workplace. Fair and equitable treatment involves more than total number of minorities and women employees. It also involves promotions, challenging assignments, good training, and other opportunities that are related to promotion.

Some important parts of NBCFAE's efforts to positively expand and promote influence in our community is providing scholarships, presenting Aviation Careers Education (ACE) camps, supporting intern programs, and establishing educational endowments. We have distributed well over $85,000 in scholarships annually to deserving students nation-wide. Over 15,000 young people have been introduced to careers in aviation at venues across this country. Those are just two examples of the ways we are moving aside the door of opposition: **"Team Work Makes The Dream Work."**

I applaud and thank NBCFAE Southern Region officers, members and our supporters for your hard work and dedication. I am pleased that this meeting will help further the important work done by NBCFAE for our members and community.

We are glad you have joined us here in Orlando. Enjoy the conference!

In Unity,
Shaun R. Sanders

From The Southern Region President

Greetings NBCFAE Southern Region members and friends,

Welcome to the Southern Region Annual Training Conference. Our theme this year "Team Work makes the Dream Work" stresses the importance of the team working together and shows that together great things can be accomplished. There are some difficult tasks ahead of us that require team work in order to achieve the desired result, our dream.

We dream of a day when everyone is actively promoting opportunities for African Americans, other minorities and female FAA employees. We dream of improvement in employee-management relations . We dream of accomplishing the goals set forth in our mission statement. Have your dreams come true? Have we accomplished our goals? If you can say yes then give yourself a pat on the back. For those who can't take that pat on the back I challenge you to join the team. With the team concept "Together Everyone Achieves More."

As part of our NBCFAE initiatives we have members spearheading the path to our dreams. Team 7 is a group of senior members of NBCFAE who have been commissioned by the National executive board to draft a plan to move the FAA towards the desired diversity in their workforce. On our behalf Team 7 is moving quickly to right the agency regarding under representation and disparate treatment. They are challenging the agency regarding illegal practices of submitting MD-715 reports that are not in compliance with EEOC regulations.

Talk to your TEAM 7 representatives and find out what you can do to help. Each of you will be asked to join us in our organization's initiatives. Educate yourself, ask questions, seek answers. We need each individual member and partner to help us reach the goals outlined in our mission, we need the TEAM.

In closing, I'd like to thank Andre and the Central Florida Chapter for all your hard work; I know it will be a great conference. I thank all of you for your support, encouragement and trust. I thank you for your elected officers that represent you on the executive board; and to the Southern Region Executive board, I say thanks for being a part of the TEAM and making the Southern Region the Number 1 region!!! I pray you'll enjoy the Conference.

In Unity,
Paquita

WELCOME

ENJOY!
CENTRAL FLORIDA CHAPTER

GREETINGS FROM YOUR CENTRAL FLORIDA PRESIDENT
ANDRE GAINES

Thank you so much for allowing us to be your host for the Southern Region Annual Training Conference. Our theme this year, Teamwork Makes the Dream work embodies the very essence of our day to day lives. Each idea begins as a dream and for that dream to become reality it takes a team of believers. Each of us in our respective roles are realities of someone's dream. The Central Florida Chapter is proud to serve as host for the 2010 Annual Southern Region Training Conference. We hope that you enjoy your visit to the "City Beautiful", the home of Walt Disney World, Universal Studios-Orlando, Sea World and The Holy Land Experience. On behalf of the officers and members of the Central Florida Chapter we welcome you with open arms.

In Unity,

Andre Gaines

OUR TEAM
SOUTHERN REGION

National
Black Coalition of
Federal Aviation Employees
Southern Region, Atlanta, Memphis,
Central Florida, Carolinas, Miami, Jacksonville,
ACE Academies, Equal Employment Opportunity,
Golf Tournaments, Basketball Tournaments, Career Days,
Employee Management Relations, College Scholarships, Newsletters

WE HOPE TO SEE YOU AT THE
34th ANNUAL NATIONAL TRAINING CONFERENCE
IN INDIANAPOLIS , INDIANA

ATLANTA CHAPTER

National Black Coalition of Federal Aviation Employees

TEAM WORK
MAKING THE
DREAM WORK

NBCFAE
National Chapter of the Year
2007, 2008, 2009

NBCFAESO.ORG

Let Each Become All They Are Capable Of Being

2010 NBCFAE
SOUTHERN REGION ANNUAL TRAINING CONFERENCE
"Dream Work makes the Team Work"

Monday, May 10, 2010

9:00am-5:00pm   Aviation Career Day

Tuesday, May 11, 2010

9:00am-7:00pm   Regional Executive Board meeting

7:00pm-8:30pm   Registration

Wednesday, May 12, 2010

8:00am-8:30am   Opening Ceremony
Master of Ceremony   Mr. Andre Gaines, President
                     Central Florida Chapter

                     Presentation of Colors
                     Oak Ridge High School USAF JROTC

                     National & Negro Anthem
                     Ms. Yasim Peoples

Opening Remarks   Ms. Robin Houdyschell
                     Destinations Meeting Manager
                     Orlando Convention & Visitors Bureau

                     Ms. Val Demings, Chief of Police
                     City of Orlando

                     Mr. Craig Chandler, District Manager
                     Air Traffic Organization, North Florida

                     Mr. Doug Murphy, Regional Administrator
                     Southern Region

8:30am-10:30 am   Air Traffic Leadership Development Program
                      Presenter: TBD

10:30 am–11:30amLeading During Times of Flux:
                      Guiding Employees through Workplace Change
                      Instructor: Patty Reyenga, Magellan Health Services

11:30am-1:00pmGeorge W. Burnette, III Awards Luncheon
(awards luncheon program enclosed)
                  Keynote Speaker: Rod C. Johnson
Greater Orlando Airport Authority

1:00pm–2:15pmCont. - Leading During Time of Flux: Guiding
                      Employees through Workplace Change
                      Instructor: Patty Reyenga, Magellan Health Services

BREAK

2:30pm-3:45pm**Resilience in the Workplace**
Instructor: Patty Reyenga, Magellan Health Services

 3:45pm-4:45pmPurposeful Productivity
                      Instructor: Patty Reyenga, Magellan Health Services

5:00pm-6:00 pm General Membership Business Meeting

Thursday, May 13, 2010

8:00am-10:00am   Coaching and Mentoring
                      Instructor: Dr. Annette Douglas, Consultant Services

10:00am–12:00pm "The Basics of Credit"
                    Instructor: Deborah Kennedy, Certified Credit
                  Counselor and Manager, Hazardous Materials Branch
                  Security Division, ASO-740

12:00pm–1:00pm   Lunch on your own

1:00pm–3:00pm   501c3 Training
Instructor: Celia Crittenden

3:00pm-5:00pm   General Membership Business Meeting

7:00pm-until   Night-out Activity
Sponsored by Central Florida Chapter

Friday, MAY 14, 2010

8:00am-11:00amGovernment Contract Solicitation Training
ARC, Eastern Region Center

11:00am–12:00pmClosing

CONGRATULATIONS
SOUTHERN REGION
ON YOUR 2010 CONFERENCE

IT'S EASY BEING GREEN!

NBCFAE JACKSONVILLE CHAPTER

In His Honor.....

NBCFAE Southern Region
George W. Burnette, III
Awards Luncheon

The National Black Coalition of Federal Aviation Employees – Southern Region has named their awards luncheon after Mr. George W. Burnette, III.

Mr. Burnette was responsible for recruiting and hiring many African Americans and other minorities into the Federal Aviation Administration (FAA) during his appointment as personnel staffing specialist in the Human Resource Management, Recruitment Branch in the Southern Region. Because of his hard work, dedication and recruitment efforts Mr. Burnette was honored at our Regional Conference in Charlotte, North Carolina on May 8, 2008. Those that were hired during Mr. Burnette's appointment could never thank him enough or put a price tag on what he did to help many the of young African Americans and other minorities enter the field of aviation. One word we can use to describe Mr. Burnette is UNFORGETTABLE, then there is AMAZING, and finally DEDICATED to helping those in need. Mr. Burnette traveled to Historically Black Colleges and Universities (HBCU's), explained to college students what the FAA had to offer and made sure they did what was necessary to get into the workforce. This and many other reasons, is why we have named our awards luncheon in honor of George W. Burnette, III. We want to let him know that we haven't forgotten his tireless journey and we as an organization are trying to walk in his footsteps. Currently we don't have the same hiring power like he did but we have the ability to go out and educate the children of the world today about the FAA and the many jobs the agency has to offer.

GEORGE W. BURNETTE, III
PRESIDENTIAL AWARDS LUNCHEON

Master of Ceremony   **Mr. William 'Moe' Moore,**   President
NBCFAE Atlanta Chapter

Welcome   **Mr. Andre Gaines, President**
NBCFAE Central Florida Chapter

Invocation   **Rev. Terrence Renard Gray**
Saint Mark AME Church
Orlando, Florida

Introduction of Special Guest Ms. Brenda C. Jackson, President
NBCFAE Miami Chapter

Lunch Served

Introduction of Keynote Speaker   **Ms. Michia Carrier**
NBCFAE Central Florida Chapter

Keynote Speaker   **Mr. Rod C. Johnson**
Manager of Public Affairs
Greater Orlando Aviation Authority

Introduction of NBCFAE   **Ms. Hannah Dixon, Vice President**
Southern Region President   **NBCFAE Southern Region**

Award Presentations   **Ms. Paquita K. Bradley, President**
NBCFAE Southern Region

Closing Remarks

Northeast Region
Congratulates
Southern Region
On the
2010
Regional Training Conference

ROD JOHNSON

MANAGER OF PUBLIC AFFAIRS
GREATER ORLANDO AVIATION AUTHORITY
Orlando International Airport
Orlando Executive Airport

Rod Johnson is Manager of Public Affairs for the Greater Orlando Aviation Authority. In this capacity, Rod is responsible for maintaining the airports high standards of communication with all forms of media.

Prior to joining the Aviation Authority, Rod was one of the most recognized and trusted news anchors in Central Florida. He helped to launch the areas first and only local 24 hour news operation, Central Florida News 13.

Rod has over 32 years of broadcast media expertise and experience, from country radio news anchor to award winning movie critic to multiple award winning journalist, Rod has won awards across the board for his professionalism and ability to tell a compelling story.

Mr. Johnson is also a former U.S. Army Military Police Officer where he served as a platoon leader and company executive officer.

Mr. Johnson is an honors graduate of Specs Howard College of Broadcast Arts. He is also an honors graduate of the U.S. Army Military Police Academy and he graduated with honors from Officer Candidate School from the Michigan Military Academy.

Rod Johnson has been an active volunteer and motivational speaker with the Orange County Public Schools and is married to his high school sweetheart. He is also the proud father of two beautiful daughters. Oh, by the way Rod is an avid movie fan from his days as a movie critic. He now owns a movie collection of well over 7000 titles.

CONNECTING NORTH AND SOUTH CAROLINA! NBCFAE CAROLINAS CHAPTER

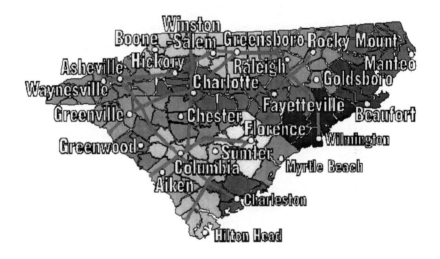

PRESIDENT......................................LYNDON MORRISON
SECRETARY.....................................HANNAH L. DIXON
TREASURER.....................................SHERIKA HOCUTT

Best Wishes from Memphis Chapter

Miami Chapter

Community Service - Provide assistance to those in need and promote careers in aviation, science and technology.

Mission Statement

We the members of the National Black Coalition of Federal Aviation Employees will promote equal opportunity for African-Americans, other minorities and female FAA employees, improve employee-management relations and provide an effective liaison among FAA employees, management and the community at large.

WWW.NBCFAESO.ORG

Index

U

W

CPSIA information can be obtained at www.ICGtesting.com
Printed in the USA
LVOW11s1702260315

431978LV00001BA/6/P